XANE

Please remember that this is a library book,
and that it belongs only temporarily to each
person who uses it. Be considerate. Do
not write in this, or any, library book.

YOUTH
UNIVERSITY
AND
DEMOCRACY

WITHDRAWN

YOUTH
UNIVERSITY
AND
DEMOCRACY

GOTTFRIED DIETZE

THE JOHNS HOPKINS PRESS
BALTIMORE AND LONDON

Copyright © 1970 by The Johns Hopkins Press
All rights reserved
Manufactured in the United States of America

The Johns Hopkins Press, Baltimore, Maryland 21218
The Johns Hopkins Press Ltd., London

Library of Congress Catalog Card Number 77-116349
International Standard Book Number 0-8018-1171-6

For
R. M.

who has lived by Voltaire's line
"mais il faut cultiver notre jardin"

CONTENTS

PREFACE

Written a troubled half-century after the publication of Max Weber's *Science as a Profession,* at a time when the University, already having been jeopardized by youthful Communist and Fascist regimes, is being challenged by youth in democracies, the present essay describes the University as a classic institution for the advancement of learning in freedom. It shows how universities, developing along with constitutionalism, have protected the freedom of the individual against authoritarian popes, kings, and popular demagogues, and urges that they continue their libertarian mission in modern democracies. That mission implies maximal benefits for the community—including youth. For only free universities can serve truth, and only advancement toward the truth can satisfy the perennial quest of a traditionally confused, sad, and brave youth for clarity and bring about the kind of public good youthful idealism has always longed for.

While I fear that the University, a reflection of classic liberalism, is on the way out as constitutional government is being replaced by unlimited, social democracy, and while I deplore present deviations in universities from the ideal University, I would also warn of unwarranted denunciations of institutions which for centuries have proved useful to the progress of learning and the pursuit of happiness.

G. D.

Baltimore
September 29, 1969

YOUTH, UNIVERSITY, AND DEMOCRACY
Introduction

Max Weber's *Science as a Profession*[1] stated many truths about the good and bad aspects of academic life. A little over a hundred years after Savigny had written on the need of his time for legislation and legal science, and about half a century after Nietzsche had despaired at the failure of the Christian churches and hoped that scholars would be willing to be martyred for the truth, this now classic essay commented on men's calling for science and on the humanistic mission of science and the university.

Weber's essay was timely. Originally a lecture to students at Munich, the city that was to become the home of National Socialism and the scene of a student revolt against the Hitler regime, it was addressed to an anxious, questioning youth that entertained strong doubts about traditional conceptions of science.

This skepticism was not surprising. Leading in Nobel laureates and considered the most scientific of nations, Germany had just lost what was then considered the most scientific of all wars. The academic youth which had enthusiastically sacrificed itself singing the *Deutschlandlied* in the battle of Langemarck, now was decimated and faced with a bleak future. Many of them must have thought of the question Franz Marc asked in a beautiful memorial occasioned by August Macke's death in action, a few months before he himself suffered the same fate: "How many terrible mutilations will this cruel war have brought upon our future culture?" As Remarque put it, here was a

[1] Max Weber, *Wissenschaft als Beruf* (1919; reprinted in *Gesammelte Aufsätze zur Wissenschaftslehre*, 2d ed.; Tübingen, 1951). The term *Wissenschaft* covers study in both the sciences and the humanities. Throughout this book, "science" must be understood in both senses.

generation that was destroyed by the war even though it had escaped its grenades. Political and economic uncertainty intensified the plight and confusion of this uneasy, erring youth. Martin Niemöller later said that at that time he and his fellow students were so restless that they could stand life in any one university for just one semester before moving on to another university. It was a time when the young desperately sought peace of mind but could not find it. After an often damned war, peace seemed to usher in the damnation of Faust.

In his answer to Weber's essay, Ernst Troeltsch could well speak of "The Revolution in Science." As he pointed out, that revolution was not confined to Germany, nor was it only the result of the war. Evident in many nations since the beginning of the century, it was accompanied in art by the *fauves* and the expressionists. It decried naturalism and intellectualism, historicism, and the specialization and relativism of dry academic routine. Its tenets were simplification and concentration, liveliness and originality, an artistic spirit, a sense for symbols, liberation from convention, and devotion to the strong personality. Paradoxically, while favoring dogma and authority, aristocracy and artistic nobility, the movement saw its main task in educating the masses. Before the Hitler movement had got under way, Nietzsche's *Bildungsrevolution* had turned into a striving for the super-humanness of all.[2]

Today again, the mission of science is paramount. Again, the good and bad aspects of academe are in focus, and one wonders how with their cult of the mediocre the universities can be as good as they are. Again, youth is in turmoil. After a second world war which saw scientific mass killings of civilians with bombs, gas, and nuclear weapons in Auschwitz, Dresden, and Hiroshima, and after a cold war interspersed with hot wars that make plain that eternal peace, often mentioned since Kant, is as far off as ever, youth again has become skeptical toward science and universities. Again, one hears about revolutions in science. But, with all the probings and suggestions for reform, it is hard to tell what everything is all about.

In many respects, the turmoil of today's youth can be compared to that of fifty years ago. Still, there are important differences. The students have changed and the turmoil has intensified. Although the students Weber addressed had just emerged from a cruel war, shattered in body and spirit and materially destitute, they usually were paying their own way and showing the discipline of the war experience. Depressed by destruction, they were eager to reconstruct; unspoiled, they

[2] Ernst Troeltsch, "Die Revolution in der Wissenschaft," *Schmollers Jahrbuch* (1921), XLV, 1003.

refrained from violence when questioning science and universities. They were still practicing the polite forms that were generally accepted by academic citizens. Although their background was less aristocratic than that of their predecessors, they were not yet the masses which are entering universities now. Reared in mass democracies, today's students are the products of the affluent society. Their studies are generously subsidized by schools and governments. Materially better off than any previous student generation, they are often spoiled and are seldom disciplined by a military experience. They often are irresponsible and violent. Spoiled, they are out to destroy "the establishment."

So many explanations have been offered for today's student unrest that one cannot help but be struck by the versatility and imagination of commentators. New and ever more sophisticated causes for student behavior are constantly discovered. The surprise and first shock over riots usually is followed by an intensive and often erratic search for causes. One investigates the conditions in the specific institution where unrest occurs and discovers faults here and there; but one often becomes aware that by no stretch of the imagination can the institution be blamed for actions such as student strikes called because parties failed to nominate acceptable candidates for the American presidency. One looks for causes outside the university. One looks at the local scene, at what is going on in the nation. One evaluates international affairs. The search is as opportunistic as it is desperate. There is no end to it. Just as all too many occasions are used by students as pretenses for unrest, all too many occasions are taken to explain unrest. The occasionalist confusion of unrest is matched by an occasionalist confusion in explaining unrest.

Other observers note certain patterns common to student riots and advance conspiracy theories. They find that most of these riots are instigated by certain types of students and by certain groups, that these groups seem to share certain ideologies and to pursue similar tactics, and that at times demonstrations take place on specific dates all over a nation or all over the world. When these observers conclude that student riots are coordinated and centrally directed, they are accused of oversimplification. If, furthermore, they maintain that direction and financing comes from Communist countries interested in undermining Western governments and that student denunciation of Communist "establishments" is nothing but a trick to broaden the appeal of the rioters and is well compatible with Lenin's recommendation of tactical retreats for the sake of strategic gains, they are decried as illiberals, Communist-hunters, and what not.

In a search for the causes of student unrest, as in any other search for truth, no explanation ought to be taken lightly as long as it is rationally advanced and not proved to be wrong. It might well contain a grain of truth, minute though it may be. Still, neither occasionalist nor conspiracy theories are wholly satisfactory. The former, all too often based upon a liberality cult and a feeling that youth can do no wrong, fail to recognize the generality of student unrest and its common pattern. They fail to examine whether and from where riots are coordinated and by whom they are directed. On the other hand, the conspiracy theories overlook that, since conspiracies generally presuppose a chance of success, there must exist conditions which form a fertile ground for subversive ideas. They do not sufficiently recognize the general malaise which makes establishments susceptible to attacks and perhaps spawns those who carry out those attacks.

It is here suggested that such a malady exists and that it exists in present "establishments." At this point, however, my opinion parts with that of rioting students: the student diagnosis of present societies is a quack diagnosis, for establishments are not sick because they are insufficiently democratic, socialist, egalitarian, etc., but for the very opposite reason—namely, because they have gone too far to the left. Student aims, therefore, are likely to increase the illness of society rather than to heal it, just as a doctor who makes a wrong diagnosis and applies the wrong therapy is likely to worsen his patient's condition. Rioting students are outcasts of the establishment only on the surface. On closer inspection, they are its products. Student rioters are outcasts of the establishment only insofar as the establishment has remained healthy. Insofar as it has become sick, they are representative of it. They are the poison produced by the infections of the body politic, out to destroy that body.

The malady of existing establishments is the political *malaise du siècle,* the replacement of limited by unlimited democracy and of liberal by social democracy—developments which are the results of the march of democracy toward mass democracy. This malaise is symbolized by the names of today's best known radical student organizations. The Students for a Democratic Society and the Sozialistischer Deutscher Studentenbund (both abbreviated SDS) demonstrate the sad truth of a democratic situation: cruelty and an increasing breakdown of law and order. Initiated in the French Revolution and forecast by de Tocqueville, the replacement of constitutional by authoritarian democracy progressed toward violence, especially after democratic legislation turned into social legislation, and eroded the respect for the traditional rule of law with its liberal content as con-

4

ceived by constitutionalists from Bracton to Dicey, from Montesquieu to Hauriou, and from von Mohl to the early Schmitt.

Max Weber was well aware of this problem. An enthusiastic promoter of democracy in Germany, he was opposed to democracy in the universities, which he obviously considered rational checks upon the emotionalism of democracy: "Democracy where it belongs. Scientific schooling . . . is a matter of the aristocratic mind." [3] A decade later, the problem was recognized by Ortega y Gasset. Having published *The Revolt of the Masses,* he emphasized a few months later the "mission of the University" as an antidote.[4] Karl Jaspers followed suit when he discussed the spiritual situation of the time shortly before Hitler democratically got hold of the German mass democracy and set out to national-socialize the universities, which in his eyes were powerful threats to totalitarianism.[5] A century after the death of Jefferson, the founder of the University of Virginia, the advocate of a National University, and the friend of a natural aristocracy who believed that education was the safest basis for popular government, the survival of the University was threatened by mass democracy. Friends of the University made it plain that the University was not to be equalized or uniformized. It was not to be a scene for politics but a haven for the pursuit of learning and the promotion of excellence. It was to be a shelter from politics.

This essential feature of the University to some degree has been lost as a result of the socialization and democratization of universities that accompanied the general growth of democracy, and this loss is a major cause of today's student unrest. Perhaps it is significant that the American democracy, in which universities were democratized earlier and more profoundly than those in other nations, witnessed the first major student revolts and that these revolts took place in Berkeley, the university of a state that did more for the social welfare of its students than any other state of the American union. In *Science as a Profession,* Weber prophesied an Americanization of science. Perhaps he implied as well the democratization of the University as the major haven of science—and the consequences of that development.

An argument against Weber's essay was that it favored a value-free science, that it separated *veritas* from *humanitas.* The following pages will examine whether perhaps Weber's approach has a greater humanizing value than has been conceded by his opponents and will attempt to demonstrate the humanistic mission of the University and its usefulness for youth and democracy.

[3] Weber, *Wissenschaft als Beruf,* 571.
[4] José Ortega y Gasset, *Misión de la universidad* (Madrid, 1930).
[5] Karl Jaspers, *Die geistige Situation der Zeit (1931)* (5th ed.; Berlin, 1932, 1953).

1

YOUTH
Search and Confusion

LONGING FOR YOUTH

Youth is in our memories and we are longing for it. As we grow older, we appreciate it more and more; its contours and contents become clearer—and dearer. The time in which we tended to idealize because we could not or would not rationalize is now viewed rationally—and itself becomes idealized. Youthful vacillating emotions now are soberly evaluated—and nostalgically thought of. Youthful actions, often eccentric, now are smiled upon with understanding. The distance in time furthers objectivity but does not totally achieve it, for we cannot free ourselves from emotion. Looking back we see a more or less pure picture which keeps us captive and which we do not want to destroy. As we grow older, we become certain of what we merely sensed in our youth, that nothing can replace experience, yet we want to cry: "Youth can!"

Who, after all, does not cherish the memories of his youth? Who does not remember that first attempt to be himself, to assert himself against his fellowmen, teachers, and parents? Who does not recall his youthful exuberance and foolishness? Who could forget youth's friendship and love, the time when he asked many questions, wanted many things, and knew and could do so little, when his responsibility was small and he could always take refuge from the harshness of life in his home? "The evil that men do lives after them; the good is oft enterred with their bones," wrote Shakespeare in Anthony's funeral oration to Caesar. In the case of youth, it seems to be the other way around: the pleasant aspects are remembered and the unpleasant ones forgotten.

James Harrington's remark that the elders could remember that they had been youth perhaps is an understatement.[1] Elders not only remember their youth, they long for it. Homer's venerable old Nestor, always wise in council, was given to exposition of the glories of his

[1] James Harrington, *Oceana* (London, 1656), 204.

7

youth. In Cicero's essay on the art of growing old, meant to praise the virtue of age, old Cato is an exceptional man who has never found old age burdensome, whereas to most old men it is so detestable that they say they are bearing a burden heavier than Mount Aetna itself. *Je suis tout réjoui de voir cette jeunesse,* wrote Racine. The Dedication in Goethe's *Faust* shows a longing for youth, as does the poet a few pages later:

> Then give me back the time of pleasures
> While yet in joyous growth I sang,
> When, like a fount, the crowding measures
> Uninterrupted gushed and sprang!
> Then bright mist veiled the world before me,
> In opening buds a marvel woke,
> As I the thousand blossoms broke,
> Which every valley richly bore me!
> I nothing had, and yet enough for youth,
> Joy in illusion, ardent thirst for Truth.
> Give, unrestrained, the old emotion,
> The bliss that touched the verge of pain,
> The strength of Hate, Love's deep devotion,
> O, give me back my youth again!

In his first lecture *On the Future of Our Institutions of Learning,* Nietzsche nostalgically thinks back to the carelessness of his youth. Seeing Strauss's *Rosenkavalier,* who would not sympathize with the Marschallin when she sadly realizes that her youth is gone? Even those whose youth was hard often long for it. We need think only of Hermann Hesse.

Our fondness of youth, however, does not remain confined to our personal lives. We like to remember, as well, the days of our country's youth. Mazzini's call for a Third Rome derived from a longing for the youth of his country—the Rome of the Caesars and of the popes. The Germans' desire for a new Reich derived from the cherished memory of previous Reichs in the youth of Germany. America, having "come of age" [2] and having advanced in years, made Americans yearn for the good days of their country's formative period. The young of civilizations have exercised a peculiar fascination. Whether or not he would agree with the statement that "almost everything that is great has been done by youth," [3] who would not admire and forgive an Alexander? Who would not think of the beauty of youth when he

[2] Cf. André Siegfried, *America Comes of Age* (New York, 1927).
[3] Benjamin Disraeli, *Coningsby* (New York, 1906), 111.

8

reads Byron, Hölderlin, or Schiller? Who would not love Vienna, an old city with one of the oldest universities? In spite of its age, this city, in which Mozart and Schubert lived, to most of us appears as a well of youth in which the Congress danced and people waltz. Edinburgh, guarded by its ancient castle, radiates the austerity of age. Yet, harboring many paintings by young artists such as Raphael and Bonington, it impresses one as youthful—a proper abode for innovators like Hume and Adam Smith.

Some trends in modern art are unmistakably motivated by the longing for the simplicity and genuineness of youthful, primitive, art.

Hippolyte Taine stated that "antiquity is the youth of the world," and throughout history, men have longed for it. We need think only of the Renaissance, of Winckelmann's praise of *edle Einfalt, stille Grösse*, of Lord Byron's dreaming in the Doric temple at Sunion of the independence of Greece, of Nietzsche's desperation that the classic world might be lost to modernity, of the continuous attempts by devoted scholars to save humanistic ideals. Even the present popularity of Greece could be prompted by a longing for the youth of our civilization. In recent times, this nostalgia became complemented by a turning to America as the most youthful of modern nations. Perhaps it is not accidental that the author of *Iphigenie in Tauris* also wrote a poem dedicated to the United States praising youthfulness. Perhaps Goethe hoped America would become a new home of the beautiful soul. Indeed, one could imagine an Iphigenia against the background of colonial architecture or the Jefferson Memorial—reminders of the classic Greek style. Could a beautiful soul also exist among the skyscrapers of the modern mammoth democracy symbolized perhaps by the Kennedy brothers who died young and to many personified good men?

THE LONGING OF YOUTH

At the same time that we long for youth, youth itself has its own longings, its dreams of greatness. Perhaps our longing results from our memory of the latter and the sad realization that the dreams of youth have not come true.

Just as Europeans have seen in the United States a rejuvenation of the old world, Americans have been longing for the realization of the American Dream. Benjamin Rush, a signer of the Declaration of Independence, a founder of Dickinson College, and the father of American medicine, spoke for many of his compatriots when he said that the newly independent nation still faced the problem of consolidating the achievements of the American Revolution and of educating the people in principles which implied an increase of the rights of the individual through an enlargement of the popular basis of government. This plan was complemented by the hope that a powerful America would bring the blessings of free government to the world. Much as the American way of life may have changed, the idea of Americanization is as strong as ever. Robert F. Kennedy's book, *To Seek a Newer World* (1967), is only one aspect of it.

The Greeks also longed to spread their ideas. Their ideal *paideia,* so well described by Werner Jaeger, was education in the Platonic sense, meaning the molding of character: education of human beings to be humane beings. Man was at the center of thought, whether we consider the Greeks' anthropomorphic gods, their concentration upon sculpturing the human form, their philosophy moving from the problem of the cosmos to that of man, their poetry with its ever-recurring theme of man and his destiny, or their *polis* as an institution which shaped man. Hoping that *paideia* would triumph, the Greeks put at the disposition of mankind the universality of their philosophy, drama, poetry, music, and gymnastics, the discipline of speech and thinking through style and science. Young Alexander's greatness may well have been due to his desire to expand the *universitas* of Greek culture, although the Greeks might have preferred spreading their anthropocentric views through erudition and peaceful discipline—a hope which Varro and Cicero transmitted to us through their concept of *humanitas.*

The longings of America and Greece are only examples of the everlasting dreams of men. The Greek achievement has been compared to the torch of Prometheus glowing among troglodytes cowering in darkness, for the Greeks discovered the principles of innovation, the moving cause of Western civilization. And with innovation came hope, the dream for a better world, and progress. Wherever there is innovation, there is hope, especially if innovation is not marred by *hybris.*

Similar as American and Greek yearnings may have been, they were, of course, quite different. Clearly, the American way of life is not and could not be that of the Greeks. But no matter how varied these and other demonstrations of cultural youthfulness may have been, they always were accompanied by hope. This does not mean that this hope always was justified. Innovators, always anticipating improvement, can also bring about deterioration. They wield a double-edged sword. On the one hand, the student of civilization admires how innovations fulfilled the hopes put in them. On the other hand, he cannot ignore how others disappointed those hopes.

In his discussion of historical crises, Jakob Burckhardt argued that the English Revolution was really not a revolution because it was not brought about by a youthful fantasy that challenged the accepted way of life. In examining the French Revolution, however, he commented: "The power of the original vision, on the other hand, is beautifully demonstrated in the *Cahiers* of 1789; its guiding principle was Rousseau's doctrine of the goodness of human nature and the value of feeling as a warrant of virtue. It was the time of flags and festivals, which saw its last brilliant moment in 1790 on the Champ de Mars. It is as though human nature, at such moments, had to give full rein to its power of hope. We are too prone to take the vision for the specific spirit of a crisis. The vision is merely its wedding finery, which must be laid aside for the bitter workaday life which follows." [4] How true this was! The exhilaration of the original revolutionaries about the coming millennium was followed by the persecution of the Girondists by their fellow-innovators, the Jacobins, in a terror which even swallowed up a Robespierre. Young Büchner's *Danton's Death* is a moving example of the disillusionment of hopeful innovators. A similar situation existed in the Russian Revolution. The hopes of the Menshevik innovators were squashed by the terror of the Bolsheviks, who in the end liquidated themselves. Pasternak's *Doctor Zhivago* is another telling story of a disenchanted innovator. According to Moeller van den Bruck and other optimistic Germans, the Third Reich was to lead a rejuvenated Germany out of the crisis of liberalism into a glorious future; however, Hitler's *Tausendjähriges Reich* was not only considerably shorter than its predecessors but was a catastrophe which even its proponents were lucky to survive.

Having mentioned some indications of the youthful spirit in the development of our civilization, I will now turn to modern youth. I shall not, however, concentrate on today's youth. Much as that generation is on our minds, such a concentration would be unduly influenced by headlines and temporary events, and any resulting evaluation might be outdated tomorrow. Rather, I plan to view the youth of our cultural epoch. This epoch, with its roots in the Enlightenment, has been influenced by philosophical schools ranging from German idealism to French-English positivism, and their twentieth-century counterparts, and by revolutions and wars. In a word, I am concerned with youth in the liberal-democratic era.

That era has been a time of youth's longing for ideals. The Enlightenment's quest for truth set free the desires of youth, inspired youth

---

[4] Jakob Burckhardt, *Reflections on History* (London, 1943), 146.

perpetually to seek new enlightenments. Onward from the brave new world of the enlightenment, youth rapidly dreamed of new worlds, discovered new heavens. Youth began moving, as if propelled by an irresistible force. Small surprise that this energy would focus on organizations, on youth movements, and that the liberal-democratic era would become an era of movements such as *Sturm und Drang* (Storm and Stress), "Young Italy," "Young Europe," nihilism, German youth movements, hippies, and the New Left.

Kant, in stating that the French Revolution "discovered in human nature an inclination and an ability to improvement," [5] seems to ignore the significant *Sturm und Drang* which preceded that revolution. Who would not be impressed by the *Sturm und Drang* started in 1770 by the twenty-one-year-old Goethe, by Herder five years his senior, and by Lenz and Klinger, who were not yet twenty? Who would not have wanted to hear the young Goethe, then a student of law at Strassburg, converse with his mentor Herder? Or to be present when he met Merck, eight years his senior and the oldest member of the group? Who would not have wanted to share the enthusiasm of the two men for Götz von Berlichingen, the "grand fellow" striving for the realization of his natural abilities? Locke, Hume, Voltaire, the encyclopedists, Richardson, Lillo, and Fielding had made explicit the challenge to traditional thought. Young, Gray, Percy, Sterne, and the Wartons had groped for a new kind of feeling. Rousseau had depicted natural man, in revolt against his time, capable of new raptures and grand desires; Rousseau's Héloise reflects a dream for the fullness of life and love. The *Stürmer und Dränger,* resenting the rigidity of burgher life, the class structure, and the refined French culture of the aristocracy, exalted the idealism of youth. The young writers dreamed of a new humanism; they exalted Shakespeare's "nature" and extolled originality and power in every aspect. Schiller's *Kabale und Liebe* and *Don Karlos* show how they fought against monarchical tyranny and for human rights. Following Rousseau, they pitted society against personal life and the inner needs of the individual. As is evident in the Gretchen tragedy, they fought for social justice and for the social outcasts. Werther committed suicide in a protest against the existing social hierarchy and socially controlled love.

Two generations later, Mazzini, at the age of twenty-six, founded the Young Italy movement. Influenced by Herder, his program also reflected the impact of romanticism and idealism, schools which followed the *Sturm und Drang* and absorbed some of its ideas. Mainly conceived as a reaction to the rationalistic and individualistic aspects

[5] Immanuel Kant, *Der Streit der Fakultäten* (Königsberg, 1798), 149.

of eighteenth-century thought, the program of the *Giovine Italia* was full of hope. Exhibiting its debt to Rousseau and Condorcet, it stood for democracy and republican government and envisaged indefinite progress. It dreamed of a new "social epoch" inspired by a new religion that would supersede obsolete Christianity. Freedom and equality would exist not only as rights but also—and here the influence of German idealism and Saint-Simon is evident—as instruments enabling the individual to perform his duties toward the group and thus to participate in the humanitarian mission of society. The unification of Italy, another dream of the movement, was to be followed by a reorganization of mankind which would associate independent republics under a single moral law. In a future epoch of humanity, economic activity would be organized on the basis of a similar association, and property would be identified with the fruit of toil. Social classes would naturally disappear.

Naturally, it seems, the Young Europe movement, founded by Mazzini in 1834, followed upon the heels of Young Italy. The new group was composed of various national "Young" movements; its dreams were outlined in 1835 in a pamphlet characteristically entitled *Faith and the Future.* Later on, Mazzini summed up his ideals in a way that betrays his faithfulness to the longings of his youth: "In eternal dignity, stands Rome. That salient point upon the horizon is the Capitol of the Christian world. And a few steps from it stands the Capitol of the pagan world. Those two adjacent worlds await a third, greater and more sublime than they, which will rise from among their ruins. This is the Holy Trinity of History, and its Word is in Rome. Tyrants and false prophets may delay the incarnation of the Word, but none can prevent its coming. Although many cities have perished, and all in turn may pass away from this earth, Rome, by the design of Providence, and as the People have divined, is the *Eternal City,* to which is entrusted the mission of disseminating the Word that will unite the world. Her life will be reproduced on an ever widening scale. And just as, to the *Rome of the Caesars,* which through Action united a great part of Europe, there succeeded the *Rome of the Popes,* which united Europe and America in the realm of the spirit, so the *Rome of the People* will succeed them both, to unite, in a faith that will make Thought and Action one, Europe, America and every part of the terrestrial globe. And one day, when the Pact of the New Faith shines forth upon the gathered peoples from the Pantheon of Humanity, which will be raised between the Capitol and the Vatican, dominating both, the age-long dissension between earth and heaven, body and soul,

13

matter and spirit, reason and faith, will disappear in the harmony of life." [6]

In the 1860's, after Compte and Marx had entered the scene, a youth movement with quite different aims came about in Russia. Known as nihilism, after the hero in Turgenev's *Fathers and Children,* its members were chiefly adolescent intellectuals allured by the movement's promise of freedom and its oversimplified solution of problems. These young disciples rebelled against the sentimentality and romanticism of their fathers. Rejecting the obligations of traditional morality, they tried to free themselves from the past. They questioned authority and every principle and ideal. Their leader, Pisarev, who was only twenty in 1860, hoped that social questions could be solved through an increasing enlightenment of the individual. He dreamed of freeing men of prejudice, piety, obligation, and allegiance to ideals. Suspicious of emotion, he considered the fine arts a futile diversion. His contemporary, Zaitzev, found art even harmful because it distracted people from the study of the natural sciences. Contemptuous of beauty and refinement, the nihilists affected rudeness in speech and manners—all in the name of the sovereign individual and the cultivation of their own personalities. They were anarchists and agnostics. Impressed by Chernishevsky's sober rationalism, they worshipped the natural sciences, hoping that these studies would destroy superstition, mysticism, and metaphysics.

If the aims of the nihilists were utilitarian, positivistic, and materialistic, the dreams of the German youth movement a generation later pursued the opposite direction. Nietzsche had denounced the mendacity of traditional standards of bourgeois behavior. Ibsen and Hauptmann did likewise in their naturalist plays which emphasized the rights of the individual as opposed to society and showed the longings of the individual for happiness. Disgusted with the stiffness and decadence of bourgeois society as it was demonstrated by Thomas Mann in *Die Buddenbrooks,* German youth rebelled against turn-of-the-century attitudes. Opposed to the materialism, conventionalism, and insincerity of Wilhelmian society, these young people dreamed of a new way of life, of beauty and liberty. *Wandervögel,* groups of young men drawn together by the warmth of emotional life, urged their fellow-citizens to escape the stuffiness of daily routine in the cities by making excursions to the meadows, mountains, and castles of the countryside, to return to nature and the genuine. They revived the folksong, folkdance, and folklore. Stefan George, who wandered to

[6] Giuseppe Mazzini, "Ai Giovani d'Italia," *Scritti editi e inediti di Giuseppe Mazzini* (Milano, 1861–91), XI, 81.

Paris where he was introduced to the circle around Mallarmé, became their poet. The *Wandervögel* longed to express the true and free individual in a new, true *Gemeinschaft* which would be a symbol of the rebirth of the nation. In this new community, freedom could become universal after a *Führer* had replaced conventional authority.

Even though many outstanding leaders of the prewar movement were killed in World War I, youth movements proliferated after the conflict. But the lofty dreams of the prewar period increasingly became centered around a regeneration of social life. Hence, the monthly *Junge Menschen,* which sought to maintain the old liberal and human spirit, did not achieve its aim. Postwar youth dreamed of discipline and authority, of submerging the individual to society, of a super *Führer* who would be followed blindly by a *Gefolgschaft* of supermen.

Today's youth movements also have their dreams—with and without narcotics. International in character and perhaps organization, they turn against the establishment in various nations. In large measure composed of the *jeunesse dorée* of the affluent society, they revolt against the very society that brought them forth. The German youth dreamed of the *Erlebnis,* or empathy—the great, unforgettable experience. Today's hippies trip into a psychedelic dreamworld. The Russian nihilists had rejected the romanticism and emotionalism of their fathers. The hippies, often neurotic and phlegmatic runaways from neurotic and phlegmatic societies, romantically and emotionally long for a modern nihilistic existence. The welfare state has "released" its children, who dream of a life of laziness accompanied by folk and soul music and poetry. In contrast to the Russian nihilists, they are indifferent to scientific achievements. In the atomic age, they have reservations about progress.

Today's more activist youth movements in many ways share the dreams of the hippies but advocate violence rather than apathy. In a way, their relationship to the hippies can be compared to the relationship in Russia of socialist radicals to nihilists. In many respects, they can also be likened to the radical German youth movements after World War I, as distinguished from the movements prior to that war. Modern youthful activists dream of violently overthrowing existing orders. They admire scientific materialism, yet they emotionally dream of a world better than that realized in the Soviet Union. They desire the emancipation of men, yet shy away from emphasizing the freedom of the individual from the government. They dream of a socialist or communist society in which everybody will be taken care of. Their heroes are communists who challenged the establishment: Rosa

Luxemburg, Karl Liebknecht, Che Guevara, Mao, Ho Chi Minh, and Dubček. Their goal is a millennium of original, pure communism.

Burckhardt felt that the French Revolution produced an "authorization for a permanent revision," declaring that "the decisively new thing which the French Revolution introduced into the world is the possibility of, and the desire for, changes for the public weal." [7] Present youth movements are true children of that revolution when they follow Herbert Marcuse and his quest for change. Many of today's youths even dream of change for the sake of change. In large measure, the longing of youth has become an automatic, soulless mechanism— an empty shell that can be filled with any content at any time. It has become devalued into something that can be everything and nothing, turn out to be good, bad, beautiful, ugly, or what have you. The often daring dreams of freeing definite values from bondage have become indiscriminate, ever-changing designs freed of all value.

THE SORROWS, RISKS, AND DANGERS OF YOUTH

We now leave the dreams to take a look at the problems of youth. For youth does not just indulge in wishful thinking. It is torn between childhood and maturity, between dreams and reality, and by harsh realities. There is probably no other age group so plagued by uncertainty, so unsure of itself, and so desperately seeking its identity. Even if this trying period does not lead youths to despair, it might well be harmful to their fellow men. "And in the morn and liquid dew of youth contagious blastments are most imminent," Shakespeare wrote in *Hamlet* (I, 3). *Jugend kennt keine Tugend.*

The dreams of the youth movements just described often turned into unforeseen realities. In a way, those dreams share the fate of the dreams of revolutionary movements which often are furthered by the young. They go up in smoke. The *Sturm und Drang*, which exalted self-destruction, deified crime, polygamy, and ecstatic insanity, developed into classicism under the guidance of the more form-conscious Goethe. On the other hand, it turned into romanticism which moved *Stürmen und Drängen* toward extremes. Herder's glorification of the folk spawned not only national movements which, as shown in Meinecke's *Weltbürgertum und Nationalstaat,* were mitigated by cosmopolitan thinking. It also originated the kind of chauvinism which made Jakob Burckhardt fearful of German unification[8] and prompted

---

[7] Jakob Burckhardt, *Historische Fragmente* (Stuttgart, 1942), 205.

[8] Letter to von Preen of July 3, 1870. *The Letters of Jacob Burckhardt,* ed. Alexander Dru (London, 1955), 140.

Nietzsche's remark in *Ecce Homo* that the Germans are *canaille*. Mazzini's program, influenced by Herder and romanticism, was brushed aside by the sober Cavour as a fantasy which appealed just to youth.[9] Yet Mussolini, an admirer of Nietzsche, was also captivated by the Young Italy movement. Significantly, the fascist anthem was *Giovinezza*. In the end, Mussolini headed the Italian Socialist Republic. Rebelling against their fathers, the Russian nihilists fathered political radicalism. Chernishevsky's politico-philosophical novel, *What Is To Be Done?*, published in 1863, was followed by Lenin's pamphlet of the same title; Lenin admired the great populist's steadfast materialism. Would the nihilists, who were intellectuals, have sanctioned the persecution of intellectuals in the Soviet Union? In Germany, the idealist *Gemeinschaft* of the youth of the Wilhelmian era was replaced by a desire to perpetuate the comradeship of the battlefield, by a quest for "fronts," "shock brigades," "storm troops," and materialistic communities. In the end, Hitler's *Volksgemeinschaft,* composed of a *Führer* and a *Gefolgschaft,* was a far cry from what youth had dreamed of. An aesthete like Stefan George, dreaming of the *Erlebnis,* would have condemned the "exciting experience" of burning books and "degenerate art," of beating and killing innocent people. We can only speculate as to the results of today's youth movements. Toynbee has ventured to predict that the hippies will bring about the end of the American way of life. Today's activists could well contribute to the end of Western civilization.

Youth movements following the Enlightenment, then, caused pains out of proportion to the evils against which they originally reacted. And these pains seem to have increased with time. The *Sturm und Drang* resulted in a nationalism which was mitigated by the cosmopolitanism of people who were educated, had a sense of measure and high ethical standards, and believed in the rule of law. Its later result, chauvinism, was more dubious, as was the legacy of the Russian nihilists. Although communist literature considers nihilism a petty bourgeois movement, it also credits it for having inspired the radicalism that brought about the Russian Revolution. The legacy of German youth movements was as disastrous, for some of these movements helped to bring about the Third Reich.

The deterioration of youth movements hardly can be due exclusively to vagueness, lack of experience, and exaggerated self-esteem. While these features characteristic of youth movements may have grown in the course of time, other factors must have been present. Po-

[9] Camillo B. Cavour, *Gli scritti del conte di Cavour,* ed. Zanichelli (Bologna, 1892), II, 43.

litical development is an important factor, and since that development was characterized by the march of social democracy, this march, perhaps more than anything else, increased the dangers of youth movements.

Youth movements remind us of romanticism, a movement in which young people, student fraternities, and such men as Bonington, Byron, Keats, Shelley, Hölderlin, Mendelssohn, and Schubert played a role. Perhaps romanticism can be considered a youth movement by definition. This is not surprising in view of the fact that it derived from the *Sturm und Drang* and, in turn, spawned youth movements. Romanticism also is as varied as youth movements and seems to defy definition. Hardly another movement has been given as many interpretations. It means different things to different people not only because it occurred in various countries and fields but also because within these fields there existed an unusual variety of interpretations. Isaiah Berlin pointed to this confusion in his Andrew Mellon Lectures and showed how hard it is to disentangle oneself from the romanticist labyrinth. Repeatedly collectivistic in outlook, romanticism frequently is manifested in a highly individualistic if not anarchistic guise. Shelley's lyrical Godwinism is paralleled by the bitter anarchism of Stirner or Bakunin. Schubert's *Lieder,* Beethoven's Promethean sonatas, Wagner's grandiloquent musical dramas, the enormous orchestrations of Berlioz—they all are romanticist, as are the pious calmness of Caspar David Friedrich and the restless motion of Delacroix. The situation is not different in literature. Romanticism ranges from the delicate poetic diction of Coleridge to the rustic language of Wordsworth, from Novalis's melopoeic phonetics to Uhland's cult of the mediaeval ballad technique and Rückert's metrical experimentation, and from Hugo and Lamartine to their critics, the Parnassians. "The element of contradiction and opposition which is encountered in romantic philosophy and aesthetics is even more pronounced in the sphere of romantic political and social theory. Not only was there a wide variety of social and political doctrines as between different schools of romanticism, but the same individual might in the course of his intellectual development embrace a succession of apparently antipodal points of view." [10]

Romanticism reflects many a dichotomy, which indicates a schizophrenic nature. Jean-Jacques, the revolutionary, satanic, and passionate enemy of society was matched by a loving, pious Rousseau who

[10] G. Ant. Borgese, "Romanticism," *Encyclopaedia of the Social Sciences* (1951), XIII, 429.

18

quietly sought solace in solitude and the contemplation of nature. In a dramatic reversal of the sexes, Madame de Staël stated this dichotomy in the persons of the passive, submissive Oswald and the active, aggressive Corinne. Balzac juxtaposed the satanic revolt of Vautrin and the Christ-like resignation of Goriot. Romanticism shows the dreams and disappointments of youth, its joy and sadness. "Exulting to Heavens, saddened to death," wrote Hölderlin, who lived a full youth and yet could not see the summer for which he was longing, perhaps because of his despair over the world. For the romanticists, hopeful joy is matched by despondent *Weltschmerz*. This *taedium vitae* can be seen in Goethe's Werther, Byron's Childe Harold, and Chateaubriand's René. The *mal du siècle,* developed by Vigny, Sainte-Beuve, Musset, and other sad young men of the nineteenth century, brought Flaubert to the verge of suicide before he was thirteen and led him to write these lines in his early anecdote, *Voyage in Hell:*

> "Will you show me your kingdom?" I asked Satan.
> "There it is!"
> "What do you mean?"
> And Satan answered:
> "The world, you see, is hell."

And yet, Goethe also created Götz; Byron, Prometheus; and Chateaubriand, Eudore. Flaubert shared the attitude of the Jeunes-France who indulged in Dionysian rituals and pseudosatanic excesses. Romanticists seem to be torn among values, seeking ideals, trying to understand themselves, and trying to find understanding from others. Already *Dialogues: Rousseau juge de Jean-Jacques* indicated this fact. Insecurity and uncertainty, often compensated for by an exaggerated self-esteem and an uncompromising consistency of idol and action, are characteristic of romanticists.

Many explanations have been given for the dichotomies of romanticism. I would follow the early Carl Schmitt and say that the main reason for those dichotomies is probably the basic "occasionality" of romanticism. As he pointed out, occasionality does not necessarily produce insecurity and uncertainty. One need think only of Malebranche's metaphysics, in which God is the final authority. However, insecurity and uncertainty are likely to come about once the individual, the genius "I," assumes all authority and becomes his own priest, his own king, his own prophet, philosopher, and poet, and his own architect in the building of his personality, and once he takes whatever he happens to notice as an occasion for his activity. And this happened in the era of romanticism. Novalis stated that in romanticism everything becomes "the beginning of an indefinite *Roman,*" a novel in which everything can happen, depending upon the *occasio* experienced by the author and his inclinations. Just as everything may become the beginning of an indefinite novel, everything may become the beginning of an indefinite poem, composition, oration, program, sentiment, dream. Everything can be the occasion for everything—with unforeseeable consequences. Everything can become an adventure. Depending upon the occasion of departure and the individuality of the romanticist, one moves—piously or demonically, quietly or enthusiastically, timidly or aggressively, and in innumerable other ways —into the realm of the limitless and intangible. The occasion may end with the fantastic. New occasions may create new worlds and new fantasies, and so it goes on and on, under the guidance of nothing but the magic hand of chance. Such an attitude would be ridiculous and impossible in other spiritual spheres and in the reality of life. In romanticism, it produces an "interesting," colorful world. To comprehend what this really means one must see not only the idylls of romanticism but also its desperation. One must see the three men whose disfigured faces stare through the colorful romantic veil, Byron, Baudelaire, and Nietzsche—three high priests who became the slaughtered victims of romanticism's private priesthood.[11]

Romanticism has always hovered over youth whether they belonged to youth movements or not. Characteristically, Eduard Spranger's study on the psychology of youth[12] is framed by poems by Hölderlin. As youth is the most romantic of ages, romanticism is the ageless companion of youth. It is the companion of today's youth. In saying this I do not mean that the young people of today share all the values of the nineteenth-century movement known as romanticism. Whereas many of these values are cherished today, our youth have new values. What I mainly have in mind is that the occasionality of the romantic era is as evident today as it was ever before—perhaps even more so. And this fact is a cause for apprehension.

In many ways a youth's lot is not an enviable one. Coming of youth in many respects is harder than coming of age. The latter means entering a legally sanctioned status which implies some certainty about one's position vis-à-vis one's fellow men. It gives one self-confidence. On the other hand, coming of youth only means crossing the thin borderline between childhood and the vague land of youth, a crossing which legally implies criminal responsibility but no civil rights. The

[11] Carl Schmitt, *Politische Romantik* (2d ed.; München, 1925), 23ff.
[12] Eduard Spranger, *Psychologie des Jugendalters* (6th ed.; Leipzig, 1926).

20

youth is not yet fully accepted by his fellow citizens. His status is not equal to theirs. He wants to be independent, yet wherever he looks he realizes that he is dependent upon parents, teachers, legislators, and so on. Youth means uncertainty, doubt, and confusion. It means pain. Coming of youth has rightly been considered a second birth.

Many a youth nostalgically looks back to his childhood. The child knows that he still belongs to the people and things that surround him. While he notices the restrictions on his ego with sadness, he does not yet know *Weltschmerz*. His inner life, the inner life of others, and the lifelessness of the world are not yet torn apart. Everything is in harmony, and there is a naive confidence in the past, the present, and the future. There is the happiness of childhood. How different is youth! The child may ask where he came from, what existed before he came into the world. The youth asks more desperate questions. He wants to know why he is, whether there is any sense in his being, and whether it might not be better if he and the world did not exist at all. He no longer considers himself part of the world that surrounds him. He is a desperate loner in a world which he does not understand and which does not understand him. There is no age in which the individual wants more to understand and wants to be more understood. There is no age in which he is more confused.

The confusion is comprehensive. It exists in space and time, with respect to the present, the past, and the future. As he grows up, the individual becomes confused about what is going on in his home, what he hears in his church and his school, or what he reads in the newspapers. As he grows into society, he comes to dislike its regulations and questions the prevalent way of life. He wonders about everybody and everything and often is desperate. He takes to *Wanderlust* to console himself. When this proves to be of no use, he seeks consolation in the assurance that his time is unusually confusing and difficult. He wanders into the "good old past," hoping to find clarity; however, he becomes aware that the past does not offer clarity either, that there are no rules to help him get his bearings. He tries religion. Confused about current religious beliefs, he may be impressed by faiths like the young Shelley's aesthetical pantheism or Mazzini's post-Christian religion, only to find out that such faiths are not the answer either. His search is anything but a pilgrim's progress and often looks like the path to Hell. He tries philosophy and law and finds that former philosophies and laws are as full of problems as present ones. He turns to ethics and becomes confused by varying standards. In aesthetics, he finds that tastes differ. In his desperation he seeks consolation in the enlightened idea that there has been a continuous progression from

21

theological-mythical thinking via metaphysics to positivism, only to shudder in the end over the latter's inhumanity and coldness. We know of Faust's desperation when after a full life of studies he recognizes that he cannot know. We can imagine how an earnest youth must feel when he comes to the conclusion that his yearning for finding his way has yielded no results in spite of his many attempts. Faust no longer had illusions. A youth thrives on illusions until he becomes disillusioned.

Uncertainty and insecurity produce a peculiar behavior. Two souls seem to live in the youth's breast. Systolic indications are followed by diastolic ones, saintly by diabolic desires. It is as if the youth had a split personality. A craving for breaking records and for excellence is followed by an incredible laziness. Exulting happiness makes room for desperate melancholy. Tenderness and cruelty, nobility and meanness, sociability and the desire for solitude, belief in authority and in revolutionary radicalism—I could name many more opposites which reflect the attitudes of youths. Mendousse speaks of an "anarchy of tendencies." [13] This condition must torment the youth. Again and again he will attempt to overcome that anarchy—and fail. Small wonder that he will try to compensate for his failures. He will become a martyr, a secessionist, an actor who experiments with characters and situations. Impressed by the heroic, the adventurous, the pathetic, and the passionate, he will be loud, nasty, and demonstrate an exaggerated self-esteem. He will show off. Youth means a search for truth but often becomes a cult of the lie. In his never-ending attempts to dispel his doubts, to prove himself, and to find his identity, the youngster, ill educated and by no means wise, tends to look upon everything subjectively—and becomes the captive of the objects he discerns. He will grab these objects and consider them occasions for furthering his good or bad ends. Like a romanticist, he wants to be his own priest.

The preceding paragraphs mirror scholars' evaluations of youth during the first quarter of this century. It is evident that at that time youth already was confused, probably more so than a generation or two earlier. This would be natural, for later generations face more value alternatives than earlier ones. As choices become more numerous and more difficult, confusion grows. *Wer die Wahl hat, hat die Qual.* Still, at the beginning of this century, there prevailed an impressive set of traditional values. Consequently, youth was not too confused. This has changed. Today's youth is faced with a veritable inundation of new values and beliefs. As a result of major changes in the economic, political, social, moral, and scientific spheres, the old

[13] Pierre Mendousse, *L'âme de l'adolescent* (Paris, 1909), 223.

22

value structure to a large extent has collapsed and is about to be replaced by a new one. To make things worse, the replacement has not yet been completed. Furthermore, what the new values will be is not yet clear. Thus, youth no longer is confronted merely with the labyrinth of the firm values of the older generation but with an enormous number of vague and ever-changing values. The traditional vagueness of youth has become complemented by the vagueness of adult life. Youth is erring in the dark more than ever before. To many young people today, the *mal du siècle* has been superseded not merely by the *fin de siècle*. They feel that the catastrophes of our century have ushered in the end of civilization. Since the age of romanticism, *Weltschmerz* has become a Leviathan.

This condition is aggravated by the fact that occasionality is more widespread than ever before. It is a characteristic feature of our time. We are aware of it every day, every hour. Whether we look at a newspaper, listen to the radio, or watch television, innumerable impressions storm into our minds. A few minutes of news—local, national, international—on politics, crime, sports, and what not, are followed by a few minutes, often only seconds, of music, advertisements, dancing, prayer, funnies, talk, song, and so on and on. The cocktail party, in which men flimsily move around superficial groups, has replaced serious discussion. The job is superseding the profession, the multiversity the university. Flirtation is ascendant over love, sex over eros, and free love over marriage, an institution which in the age of divorce has become more and more transitory. We have become insecure in the crowd, erratic followers of slogans. We have lost our roots. We have become wanderers who go from station to station, only to be disappointed again and again. We are torn between isms and destroyed by schisms. In 1897, after the pleasant illusion of impressionism, Gauguin asked, "Where do we come from? What are we? Where do we go?" They became the desperate questions of our century. After van Gogh shot himself, the expressionists depicted men and their surroundings in the desolation of human existence; however, in their works one still can recognize men and matter. Who can now that abstractionism has led us into a no man's land? We not only suffer from an opportunistic use and abuse of values. We see values in things that have little value and in an opportunistic way make the most of them.

And where is youth—confused by definition—in this turmoil that brings desperation even to disciplined, mature adults? Their confusion must have grown immensely—and with it, their potential threat. For the growth of uncertainty and insecurity is likely to increase the desire to compensate. During *Sturm und Drang* and romanticism, *Welt-*

23

schmerz drove youth to suicide and mild reforms. Youth today go beyond that. The dreams of youth have been replaced by fantastic obsessions. Mild reforms have been superseded by wild plans, the thought of suicide by that of murder. If God is dead, why not the world?

YOUTH, EDUCATION, AND DEMOCRACY

The dangers of youth have always been recognized and prompted educational measures. Aristophanes, considering himself a youthful rebel against the sophistic corruption of his time, has given us a debate between philosophy and sophistry, in which Philosophy says:

> Gentlemen,
> I propose to speak of the Old Education, as it flourished once
> beneath my tutelage, when Homespun Honesty, Plainspeaking, and
>   Truth
> were still honored and practiced, and throughout the schools of Athens
> the regime of the three D's—DISCIPLINE, DECORUM, and
>   DUTY—
> enjoyed unchallenged supremacy.
>   Our curriculum was Music and
>   Gymnastic,
> enforced by that rigorous discipline summed up in the old adage:
> BOYS SHOULD BE SEEN BUT NOT HEARD. This was our
>   cardinal rule,
> and when the students, mustered by groups according to region,
> were marched in squads to school, discipline and absolute silence
> prevailed.
>   Ah, they were hardy, manly youngsters. Why,
> even on winter mornings when the snow, like powdered chaff,
> came sifting down, their only protection against the bitter weather
> was a thin and scanty tunic. In the classes, posture was stressed
> and the decencies firmly enforced: the students stood in rows,
> rigidly at attention, while the master rehearsed them by rote,
> over and over. The music itself was traditional and standard—
> such familiar anthems and hymns as those, for instance, beginning
> *A Voice from Afar* or *Hail, O Pallas, Destroyer!*—and the old modes
> were strictly preserved in all their austere and simple beauty.
> Clowning in class was sternly forbidden, and those who improvised
> or indulged in those fantastic flourishes and trills so much in vogue
> with the degenerate, effeminate school of Phrynis, were promptly
>   thrashed
> for subverting the Muses.
>   In the gymnasium too decorum was
> demanded.

24

The boys were seated together, stripped to the skin, on the bare ground
keeping their legs thrust forward, shyly screening their nakedness
from the gaze of the curious. . . .

                                 At table courtesy and good manners
were compulsory. Not a boy of that generation would have dreamed
of taking so much as a radish or the merest pinch of parsley
before his elders had been served. Rich foods were prohibited,
raucous laughter or crossing their legs forbidden. . . .[14]

Philosophy's ideal of education, then, was characterized by discipline, decorum, and duty. This *paideia* was generally accepted by the
Romans, who believed in the principle, "a healthy mind in a healthy
body." Basically sanctioned by the Church, it prevailed until the Enlightenment as "humanistic" education. Since then, it has been superseded by educational methods which put less emphasis upon those
values. Goethe, judging the two children of *Sturm und Drang,* felt that
classicism was healthy and romanticism, sick. For him, disciplined,
decorous *Mass* was preferable to the undisciplined, occasional mess of
Schwärmerei. Educators, on the other hand, increasingly followed the
man who has been considered the father of romanticism—Rousseau.
Known also as the father of modern democracy, he stands in the middle of educational reforms between John Locke and John Dewey, the
former living at the beginning of constitutional democracy in England
and the latter at the beginning of absolute democracy in the United
States.

After the efforts of Rabelais, Montaigne, Bacon, and Comenius,
John Locke became the major spokesman for a new conception of education in a revolt against the highly disciplinary methods of the "hu-
manists." Advancing most of his ideas in *An Essay Concerning Human
Understanding* (1690) and *Some Thoughts Concerning Education* (1693),
Locke considered discipline a prerequisite to the physical, moral, and
intellectual development of the individual. Believing that a sound
mind could best flourish in a sound body, he formulated strict rules
for body culture: frequent cold baths, open air, light clothing, frugal
meals, early to bed and on a hard bed, and plenty of exercise. Discipline of the body was to be complemented by moral discipline: immediate and willing obedience to elders, self-control and self-denial, to
be enforced, as a last resort, by corporal punishment. Great impor-

---

[14] Aristophanes, *The Clouds,* trans. William Arrowsmith (Ann Arbor, 1962), 73f. The
permission of the University of Michigan Press to reprint is appreciated.

tance was placed on good breeding. The formation of character and a fine personality were more important than the cultivation of mere intellectual faculties. It cannot be denied that Locke's emphasis on discipline, virtue, wisdom, breeding, and learning comes close to the classic, humanistic ideal of education. And yet, the philosopher of the American Revolution made inroads upon that ideal. Subordinating comprehensive learning from books to down-to-earth things such as reading, writing, and arithmetic, and subordinating the study of Latin to French and the mother tongue, Locke's educational method was mainly geared to preparing the young for practical life. It was likely to prevent an acquaintance with philosophy and humanistic values. It reduced discipline by the sheer fact that it no longer required discipline for the learning of "non-practical" matters. It hampered education in the sense of *paideia* and made it harder for the youth to strike philosophical roots, to gain clarity, to find his bearings, to become a humane, as distinguished from a mere human, being. It was likely to make him a mere object of, and adjuster to, the occasions of daily routine, an opportunistic and confused errand boy.

This possibility increased with Rousseau's *Émile* (1762). Believing that everything degenerates in the hands of man, the philosopher of the French Revolution left education to nature itself. Placed under the care of a tutor about his age, Émile grows up a healthy animal. Far removed from society, he yields to no authority but that of his own instincts. He never is forced to do anything he does not wish. He is not taught by his tutor who merely shelters his free development. His own experiences teach him what is wise and good, what leads to success and what to failure. Body and mind grow naturally in various stages. Having developed a strong body, Émile obtains most of his intellectual training. He engages in practical studies, in scientific orientation, manual labor, and excursions into nature. One discovery leads to another. In time, learning becomes more systematic because the youth learns to judge and reason. At eighteen, the "age of humanity," Émile's social and moral education intensify through historical studies and the reading of fables. He now can be exposed to religious questions so that he may freely choose a religion. At twenty, he engages in more refined studies. He learns Latin, Greek, and Italian and reads drama and poetry in their original tongues. He becomes a gentleman, able to head a household and to be a distinguished citizen. His moral values will be relative to need, time, and place. In a word, they will be determined by the occasions of daily life and routine. Like Locke's youth, Rousseau's youth is supposed to adjust himself to fleeting, temporary values. Since a humanistic education from the twentieth year on can hardly make up for the earlier neglect of humanistic studies, Rousseau's youth is likely to be as confused as Locke's. As a matter of fact, he probably is worse off. Whereas Locke, discouraging humanistic studies, had only decreased discipline, Rousseau largely eliminated it. Putting his trust in a dubious self-discipline of children and youngsters, he left an unstable youth lonely in a corrupt society.

In spite of their lightening of discipline, Locke and Rousseau could still hope to approach the humanistic ideal of *paideia*. They believed in the existence of fixed ideas and considered education a means to achieve some kind of humanistic, genuine virtue which could aid youths' orientation and provide them with confidence. For John Dewey, who wrote at the height of American democracy, there are no fixed beliefs. He considered the search for certainty a "compensatory perversion" [15]—an illusion which diverts men's attention and abilities from the possible and practical realities within their comprehension. He subordinated the end to the means and even abolished the distinction between them. Life is meaningless, the aimless life is to be commended. The same principles of explanation apply to animal and human life. There is no realm of ends. Everything is provisional. Change is a fruitful category. The act precedes the thought. Small wonder that Dewey became an advocate of an educational method which negates discipline and permits the child to drift according to his instincts and desires. The youth Dewey had in mind is surrounded by nothing but provisional values. He finds himself living in a world in which every value is as provisional and as important as every other—a world composed of provisoria which are equally inadequate. Robert Hutchins summed up this situation: "Today the young American comprehends only by accident the intellectual tradition of which he is a part and in which he must live . . . holding that nothing is any more important than anything else, that there can be no order of goods and no order in the intellectual realm. There is nothing central and nothing peripheral, nothing primary and nothing secondary, nothing basic and nothing superficial." [16] On the face, it looks as if this conglomeration of equalities would put youth at ease. If all things are equal, then accepting one must be as good as accepting another. If nothing is better than anything else, nothing can be worse than anything else. *Weltschmerz* must lose its rationale. But this is not the way it works. Equalities exclude values, and youths are desperately looking for values. They will be disappointed when they find nothing. When an empty world stares into their face, they will stare back and ask the old question: "Why am I and why is the world?" The product of "progres-

[15] John Dewey, *The Quest for Certainty* (New York, 1929), 228.
[16] Robert M. Hutchins, *Education for Freedom* (Baton Rouge, 1943), 25f.

sive education," an undisciplined and spoiled youth sooner or later must fall into complete confusion. Dewey's *The Way out of Educational Confusion,* published in 1931, fifteen years after his *Democracy and Education,* indicates the dilemma which his educational theories helped to bring about.

It sometimes is argued that the increasing loss of discipline in education could be compensated for by compulsory public education, which came about in most nations after the eighteenth century and received its greatest boost during the French Revolution. Indeed, it is conceivable that a guaranteed minimum of education for a large part of the population might have prompted a lessening of discipline. Perhaps there is significance in the fact that Locke, a disciplinarian, was lukewarm about public education; that Rousseau, less disciplinarian, wanted it; that Dewey, not disciplinarian at all, took it for granted. It appears doubtful, however, that the imposition of education upon more and more people justifies less and less discipline in education, for it basically amounts to an expansion of quantity at the cost of quality. And this is too high a price to pay. Whereas education is desirable for as many people as possible, it must remain genuine education and not become diluted. "Education for all is no education at all" is a specter which cannot be dismissed lightly. Public education, then, did not alleviate the basic decline of education even if we see public education at its best and discard the warning of John Stuart Mill's article "Endowments" that, if permitted to replace private education, public education would mold all men into the same intellectual pattern.

In answer to Mill's fear, disciplinarians will argue that such molding is exactly what the young need if they are to be delivered from confusion and despair and to be brought to clarity and hope. Others will add that such a molding must be especially effective if it is favored by, and in turn favors, the new deities which in modern times have replaced the church, such as nationalism, socialism, and democracy.

We can dispose of the former two easily. Our interest is in the free education of men to be free men, and both nationalism and socialism have hardly proved to be conducive to this aim. While the nationalism of a Fichte or a Mazzini was compatible with the humanistic idea which at that time was threatened by Napoleon and British imperialism under the slogan, "my country, right or wrong," German and Italian nationalism later degenerated into the opportunism of Hitler and Mussolini. Under their regimes nationalism no longer was disciplined by humanism but disciplined humanism out of existence. As to social-ism, a dictatorship of the proletariat, or of those who pretend to speak for it, is incompatible with true education. It also has been shown that forms of socialism that are mitigated, or disciplined, by liberal democ-racy lead to serfdom.[17]

Our hope, then, rests upon democracy. Could the growth of democ-racy make up for the loss of discipline in education? Could democracy have become an ideal so overpowering that it would instill the young with so great a devotion, give them so great a sense of belonging and direction, as to alleviate the risks and dangers of youth? Is there sig-nificance in the fact that Locke, hoping for limited democracy, still believed in disciplinary methods; that Rousseau, desiring a less lim-ited democracy, believed in "negative education"; that Dewey, seeing the actual progression in the United States from limited to unlimited democracy, favored "progressive education"? Did democracy beware of the pitfalls of nationalism and socialism? Did it remain disciplined by humanism in order that men might be freely educated to be free? Without much doubt, this had been the hope of democratic educators. Locke the student of Coke, Rousseau the contemporary of Condorcet, Dewey the student of Jefferson—they all felt that popular government should provide for the rights of man and thus be limited, or disci-plined, by those rights. They all hoped that democratic development would make democracy a safer and safer haven for *paideia.* Increasing participation by the individual in government would result in increas-ing emancipation of the individual from government. The individual's freedom would not be the freedom of anarchy but the freedom under the rule of law. Education for a liberal democracy in a liberal democ-racy would bring clarity to the mind of youth, give hope to youth, and eliminate the dangers of youth.

In the last analysis, this hope was based upon the speculation that liberal democracy would remain free of the occasionality characteris-tic of romanticism. It was a vain hope. To begin with, democracy has a romantic burden, for it was tied up with historical romanticism. Rousseau, the father of modern democracy, was also a father of ro-manticism. Even after Jacobin democracy and Napoleon's democratic caesarism had made room for a more liberal democracy, democracy remained connected with romanticism. As a matter of fact, democ-racy can be said to be the *alter ego* of romanticism. As late as the 1870's, Taine considered romanticism a bourgeois movement against the aristocratic rule of the eighteenth century, a democratic revolt at a time when the human mind was becoming *plus capable d'abstraire,* a

[17] F. A. Hayek, *The Road to Serfdom* (Chicago, 1944).

29

revolt which denounced traditional forms as artificial and searched for the truthful and natural—often at the cost of all form. When speaking of democracy, he had in mind the then existing liberal democracy, a democracy that found its purpose and limits in the rights of man, a democracy which the bourgeoisie in 1789 created in a revolution against the aristocracy and in 1848 defended against the proletariat. Romantically, Taine hoped that romanticism would bring about a new order—but feared that it would end in chaos.[18]

Events have shown that Taine's fears were more justified than his hopes. The leadership of democracy, at his time basically confined to an educated bourgeois élite, has since been transferred to the less educated masses. Whereas the liberal democracy of the romantic era was largely determined, as Taine put it, by the *plébéien occupé à parvenir,* modern democracy became more and more the domain of plebeian parvenus. The revolution of the bourgeoisie has been superseded by the revolt of the masses.[19] Now this development does not necessarily prevent the creation of a new order. It is probable that the masses in their own democratic order will be run by their kind or by a demagogue representing them—who like Stalin, Mussolini, or Hitler may well be a plebeian parvenu. No one would doubt that this would constitute an order, if only an order in which people stew in their own juices. Such an order, however, is likely to be so authoritarian and so incompatible with a humanistic education that we need not elaborate on it. What is of interest to us is democracy as it exists in Western nations. Whereas some of these democracies perhaps have already reached the stage of absolute majority rule, there are still liberal elements present in them to qualify them as potential havens for humanism. Regrettably, these democracies not only have failed to achieve the order which Taine hoped they would but have become increasingly formless. Modern mass democracy, being less rational than the élitist liberal democracy of the nineteenth century, has become confused and confusing, in spite of the fact that the most "confusing" innate aspects of liberal democracy, divisions of power, in large measure have been discarded.

Modern democracy has become an empty shell to be filled with the contents various occasions may demand and to be emptied again on new occasions. We need think only of campaign promises which are forgotten after elections and replaced by new promises directed toward winning coming elections. Modern democracy in large measure has become an opportunistic race to influence those naive recepta-

[18] Hippolyte Adolphe Taine, *Histoire de la littérature anglaise* (3d ed.; Paris, 1873–74), IV, 233ff.

[19] José Ortega y Gasset, *La rebelión de las masas* (Madrid, 1929).

30

cles of wishful thinking, the voters' brains. Or consider the decline of that traditional stronghold against confusion and uncertainty—the law. Everything seems fit to be poured into legal forms today. Modern legislators seem to be obsessed with revising old and making new laws. Worse still, legislative acts increasingly have become complemented by executive rules and regulations. In view of this inundation with laws and regulations, I asked a few years ago whether the "motorized" lawmaker, noticeable since World War I, is not about to be replaced by the "jet" lawmaker.[20] Today, the situation is worse still. The opportunistic attitude of lawmakers has been followed by opportunistic attitudes of judges, who are obviously reluctant to enforce the law in a way that would secure law and order. This has resulted in an increasing disregard for the law and in the deplorable breakdown of law and order which has occurred in the past years in the major democratic nations. As can hardly be otherwise, the decline of the law was accompanied by a decline of morals, which are in a state of confusion and are rapidly approaching a complete breakdown. Many of these aspects of modern democracy still are concealed by facades, but these facades only enhance the basic deceit of our time. And woe to the youth who looks behind them!

If a youth hopes to find a democracy similar to that described in Pericles' Funeral Oration, a way of life which provided *paideia* in a firm order, he will see instead humanistic ideas trampled by neurotic and inconsiderate masses in an environment that approaches chaos. Instead of Winckelmann's "noble simplicity, silent grandeur," he will find vulgar pomposity and loud pettiness. Instead of a refined democracy, disciplined for the sake of the individual by divisions of power, he will encounter a coarse and undisciplined majority rule which has discarded constitutional safeguards and indulges in abuses of power. He finds political science replaced by politics. He will become aware that the noble citizen, who took the place of the noble savage and defended democracy, has been pushed aside by the savage citizen, the petty bourgeois. He becomes convinced that the voice of the people cannot possibly be the voice of God.

This, then, is the lot of youth today. Rather than ameliorating the confusion natural to youth, modern democracy has enhanced it and has increased youth's desperation. Born with romanticism, democracy has reduced romanticism to its skeleton of occasionalism, to its bare, value-free essentials. Youth in the era of romanticism still saw ideals, beauty, and harmony around themselves, ideals which could make them forget the occasionality of their time. Today's youth, while they

[20] See the author's *In Defense of Property* (Chicago, 1963), 152.

31

like to dream on, see themselves surrounded by materialism, ugliness, and disharmony and are constantly aware of life's occasionality. Youths in the romantic era committed suicide out of *Weltschmerz*. Today's youth strikes out against the painful world. The romantic youth basically was gently passive. Today's youth is unseemly active; however, their activism is likely to increase their confusion and desperation. Schiller's *Räuber* knew what they wanted. Today's youth are too confused to know what they want. They want to have a voice in everything, but their voice betrays indecision. It adds another dimension of confusion to a society that already is confused and fast moving into the turbulence of anarchy and collapse.

2

UNIVERSITY
Research and Clarity

UNIVERSITY AND DEMOCRACY

In the turbulence of modern democracy, the idea of the university must stand out as a ray of hope. The *sapientia universitatis* must emerge as a welcome check upon the *confusio multitudinis* of the pluralistic society. An institution which embodies the fusion of the sciences must be greeted as an antidote to the confusion of popular opinions. The unity of learning must be hailed as a replacement of the occasionality of the people's daily routine. *Lux et veritas:* as the torch of Prometheus let the troglodytes see the truth, universities could shed light and bring truth into a democratic world which has become increasingly obscure and false.

Universities are the opposites of modern democracies in many respects.

The constituents of democracies are citizens; those of universities are academic citizens. Democratic communities are composed of the mass of the people; universities, of a fraction of that mass. Democracies are egalitarian; universities, élitist. These basic distinctions have prevailed to our day. Whereas more people are in universities now than ever before, more people also participate in the democratic process. The growth in the number of academic citizens has not substantially affected the élitist character of universities.

The aim of universities is the search after truth; that of democracies, convenience. When pronouncing the principle *salus populi suprema lex esto,* Cicero may well have shared the belief that the welfare of the people only can exist in truth. However, while this belief recognizes the possibility that the people will rise toward the search of the truth, the chances are that their aims will be of a less exacting nature. Even Cicero felt that the search after truth would come only after physical wants have been satisfied.[1] One can dispute the idea expressed in Hegel's *Philosophy of Law* that the people do not know

[1] Cicero, *Offic. init.*

33

what they want.[2] They know pretty well what for the time being is convenient for them. Marx regretted that the people are unwilling to make sacrifices for a revolution. Be that as it may, they generally are unwilling to make sacrifices for the search after truth. They like to consume, but are unable to create, the fruits of research.

Universities, while not immune to emotion, are strongholds of rationality. Modern democracies, while not devoid of rational features, in a large measure have become theaters of emotions. Whereas democracy could be a rational form of government—and was so conceived by its modern founders in England, the United States, and France according to principles laid down by such men as Coke, Locke, Montesquieu, and the authors of *The Federalist*—modern democracies, having become mass democracies, have tended toward emotionalism and irrationality. By the time of Ortega y Gasset, de Tocqueville's fears had been borne out. Ariosto's and Goethe's skepticism toward the rationality of the masses,

Che'l volgare ignorante ogn' un riprenda
E parli più di quel che meno intenda.

Zuschlagen kann die Masse,
Da ist sie respektabel;
Urteilen gelingt ihr miserabel,

appears to have been more justified than the neutralism Hegel expressed at a time when men still harbored great hopes for rational democracy.[3] On the other hand, due to the advance of the natural sciences and their research methods, universities have become more, rather than less, rational. Even Ortega, critical as he was of modern universities, recognized them in his *Mission of the University* as strongholds of rational behavior which stood in sharp contrast to the irrationality of modern mass rule.

Democracies have become unstable. Universities have remained relatively stable. It is true that in recent years universities have been faced with problems of stability; nevertheless, instability in universities is still exceptional. By contrast, instability has become the rule in modern democracies in spite of the survival of various stability factors. Having often been plagued by instability (the cities of ancient Greece and the American states under the Articles of Confederation are examples), democracy in the twentieth century has tended toward

---

[2] Georg Wilhelm Friedrich Hegel, *Sämtliche Werke* (Stuttgart, 1949), VII, 409. See also 383f., 413f.

[3] *Ibid.,* 425.

instability on account of the irrationality of politics and the growing elimination of checks upon those in power. Democratic governments change fast according to popular whims and desires. University tenure regulations prevent a frequent turnover of personnel. To please their constituents, democratic governments increasingly have engaged in changing the laws. With a few exceptions, universities have observed time-honored customs, rules, and regulations. Paraphrasing Coke's distinction between natural and artificial reason,[4] it could be said that in democracies the natural reason of the citizens can always determine what the law is and what it ought to be. On the other hand, the natural reason of academic citizens always is under the rules and regulations of science, under some kind of artificial reason which has been compiled by great minds over generations.

Modern democracies have become challenges to law and order. In spite of outbreaks of violence on several campuses, universities generally have retained their laws and orders. The predicament of democracies is not surprising, for it follows from the natural instability of democracy. As long as constitutions were recognized as supreme laws controlling democratic processes, the issue of law and order could not easily arise. It was bound to arise when constitutions were no longer unequivocally so recognized, and when, due to the march of democracy, the contents of constitutions became determined by legislation or judicial adjustment. Constitutional legitimacy was replaced by a mere legality under which rulers could transmute into law ideas that could challenge law and order.

Finally, modern democracy has accepted equality for its faith, whereas universities have continued to believe in liberty. In the democratic revolutions in England, the United States, and France, democracy was conceived as a liberal democracy in which equality meant equality before laws which permitted the free use of unequal abilities. In modern times, de Tocqueville's prediction that the march of democracy would move toward egalitarianism has been borne out. The primacy of liberty increasingly has become replaced by that of equality. The latter no longer means equality before the law but equality through the law. This development has not taken place in universities. While universities are more egalitarian today than previously because the influx of students has led to a certain levelling of requirements, universities in general still emphasize the free development of the individuals' unequal abilities over the equal development of all.

If one looks for a common denominator in the features which dis-

[4] *Coke on Littleton*, § 97b.

35

tinguish modern universities from democracies, one could say that it is clarity. In contrast to convenience, the major aim of democracies, the inherent aim of universities, truth, implies clarity. *Wahrheit, Klarheit; Klarheit, Wahrheit.* Characteristically, truth is depicted as a nude holding a mirror clearly showing herself.[5] If truth means clarity, then an academic community, devoted to the search for truth, must reflect greater clarity than a community of ordinary citizens, who are primarily interested in the enjoyment of the Garden of Eden—a veritable labyrinth of the conveniences of daily life. There cannot be much doubt that rationality is clearer than emotions, that there is greater clarity in stability than in instability, that law and order represent clarity better than anarchy and disorder. Also, liberty is clearer than equality. It stands out in an egalitarian environment, an environment which usually is devoid of clarity. Furthermore, it is questionable whether in an egalitarian environment, tending as it does toward passivity, there can be achieved as much as in a libertarian one, conducive as it is to activity.[6]

UNIVERSITY, TRUTH, AND REASON

Clarity factors in today's universities reflect the original idea of the university. They exist because throughout history universities, while never absolutely realizing the ideal University, have done their best to approach it. To Hegel's dictum, "what is reasonable is real; and what is real is reasonable,"[7] can be added that what is, in large measure is reasonable because universities have upheld the idea of the university. Hegelian reasoning might not have achieved its dominating position had not friends of the idea of the university, Wilhelm von Humboldt, Fichte, Schleiermacher, and Steffens, helped to found the University of Berlin. In turn, that university never could have been founded had not the idea of the university been kept alive and had universities not successfully defended that idea against outside encroachments.

In his lecture "On the Calling of the Scholar," delivered at the University of Jena shortly after the French Revolution, Fichte considered the scholar "a priest of the truth," a man committed to do, dare, and suffer anything for the truth, willing to be persecuted, hated, and even

[5] "Hinter dieser Augen Klarheit/ruft ein Herz in Lieb' und Wahrheit"—Goethe./ "Du weisst, Betrug und Tand umringt die reine Wahrheit/verfälscht ihr ewig Licht und dämpfet ihre Klarheit"—Haller.

[6] See the author's *In Defense of Property*, esp. 139ff.

[7] Hegel, *Philosophy of Law*, 33.

36

to die in its service.[8] He had in mind a personality quite different from the occasionalist romanticist who was his own priest, who would announce and arrange his own truths or half-truths, and often advertise them as the only undisputable truth. He had in mind the kind of hero Nietzsche wanted—a man willing to be martyred for the truth. Unequivocally committed to the search for truth, the University was to be a rock of trustworthiness and a symbol of clarity.

We may well maintain that it is. Truth, of course, may cause pain. Still, the saying, "who increases knowledge, increases pain," is dubious. The very fact that there is truth gives us assurance. Truth provides security because it is indestructible. Truth gives confidence: "When the world is about to drown, it must be saved through a revelation of truth" (Mong Dsi). Truth encourages: once we have sensed it, we want to search for it restlessly, hoping that the mind will find peace through its discovery.[9]

Pilate's question "What is truth?" suggests that there is no such thing. Indeed, this question has been answered in such a variety of ways that doubts about the existence of truth seem to be justified; however, the question has been answered in a variety of ways only because men are fallible. From an objective point of view, there can be only one truth, although men may not know what it is. Goethe, who wrote Reinhard "that the various modes of thinking are rooted in the differences of men and for this reason a general uniform conviction is impossible," still wrote in "Zahme Xenien":

> Wenn ich kennte den Weg des Herrn,
> ich ging' ihn wahrhaftig gar zu gern;
> führte man mich in der Wahrheit Haus,
> bei Gott! ich ging' nicht wieder heraus.

The fact that men are unable to discover the truth does not prove that it does not exist.[10] Errors prove the existence of truth. *Error multiplex, veritas una.* Intellectual history is a history of discovering errors and replacing them by truths, a continuous diminution of error, a neverending progress toward truth. Perhaps Pilate sensed this. His question, while revealing doubts whether men can know the truth, also reveals hope in the existence of truth. Whereas men may not know the truth, they may strive toward knowing it. In the last analysis, their search

---

[8] Johann Gottlieb Fichte, *Über die Bestimmung des Gelehrten* (1794), in *Sämmtliche Werke,* ed. J. H. Fichte (Berlin, 1845–46), VI, 333f.

[9] Karl Jaspers, *Von der Wahrheit* (München, 1947), 453.

[10] See *ibid.,* 733; Max Scheler, *Der Formalismus in der Ethik und die materiale Wertethik* (4th ed., Bern, 1954), 70, 204.

cannot be disappointing. It may often yield few results. It may be difficult and frustrating. *La vérité ne se découvre qu'avec peine.* Still, there always will be satisfaction in having progressed a little further toward one's aim, and even the awareness of errors will result in a pride for having advanced.

The search for the truth has been given high ranking throughout the history of Western civilization. Cicero considered it the most important intellectual endeavor. The passage where he mentions this is, according to Cardinal Newman, but one of the many similar passages by a multitude of authors.[11] Serving the truth has generally been considered the major aim of the University, from its inception in ancient Greece to the studies of Jaspers and Ortega and others in our era.

The University's aim for clarity, following from its commitment to the search after truth, is enhanced by the way it goes about that search. There can be no doubt that many a truth has been discovered by mere speculation. Without speculation there is no advancement of learning; however, even the results thus found are accepted only upon scientific verification. The search for the truth is a scientific pursuit. Its aim for clarity is advanced through clear methods.

Implying clear methods to attain the clarity of truth, science has certain assumptions. The slogan "science assumes nothing" is justified only insofar as science cannot admit any restrictions upon its advancement. It must be skeptical not only toward such things as religions and *Weltanschauungen* but also toward generally accepted beliefs, even if they are held by respected scientists. *Vérité dans un temps, erreur dans un autre,* wrote Montesquieu. Science refuses to accept anything as an absolute truth, just as it refuses to consider anything unworthy of scientific investigation. Science assumes that nothing limits the scope of inquiry. Scientific inquiry is endless. The scientist is a Faustian by definition. *Wer immer strebend sich bemüht, den können wir erlösen,* the angels sing when they admit Faust into Heaven. In the lecture referred to, Fichte said that the scholar as the servant of science must forget what he has done as soon as it is done and think only of what else there is to be done. Science is ruthless. It takes on Gods, it deprives saints of their haloes. It destroys the myth of popular heroes. It challenges the results of scientific investigation. As a priest of the truth, the scientist is without mercy. Unlike the blindfolded eyes of *Justitia,* his eyes are wide open, always looking to find fault and to condemn. Obsessed with discovery, he need not care about consequences. Sir Arthur Fleming discovered penicillin, and Otto Hahn split the uranium atom, opening the way for unforeseen blessings and

[11] John Henry Cardinal Newman, *The Idea of a University* (New York, 1947), 92f.

destructions. In good faith, leading scientists awarded the Nobel Prize, made possible by the inventor of dynamite, to both. Destroying and building, the scientist provides the dynamics of learning.

Scientific research assumes daring. It assumes that the scientist let himself be guided by the "schemes of ideas" Kant had in mind, by ideas and hypotheses which might enable him to gain new insights— often by pure chance. He must offer the discovery of truth a chance, remote as it may be, even though the chances of coming closer to the truth by mere daring may be slim. While scientific work presupposes daring, it also assumes that the scientist determine the direction and scope of his investigation. Furthermore, it assumes that he is open to criticism. The scientist cannot deny the principle of contradiction. As a search for the truth, science presupposes the validity of the rules of logic. The scientist controls his plans and is controlled from the outside. His daring and devotion are complemented by discipline.

The latter is related to what has been considered inseparable from and the equivalent of science—method. Complementing the approaches of Grotius, Hobbes, Spinoza, Pufendorf, and Wolff, Descartes, in his *Discours de la méthode,* gave classical advice for research in clarity: resolve every problem into its simplest elements; proceed by the smallest steps so that each progress of the investigation may be apparent and compelling; take for granted only what is perfectly clear. These remarks, which Descartes believed to be generalizations of the process by which he had discovered analytical geometry, were similar to those one finds in Galileo's dialogues on mechanics. The method proposed came to be applied by scientists generally. The deductive method was complemented by the inductive method. Characteristically, the discovery of new scientific truths was matched by an ever-increasing invention of new names and types of methods. But irrespective of whether scholars have felt that a method was, or should be, regressive, analytical, progressive, synthetic, systematic, heuristic, genetic, critical, dialectic, akroamatic, erotematic, and what not, there has always existed consensus concerning the necessity of some kind of method, suited to the subject-matter to be investigated. *Methodenstreit* has not disparaged but aided method. Mere guesswork or planless attempts which result from subjective ideas and mere whims have been generally rejected.[12]

Methods contribute to the cogency of scientific knowledge, which exists on account of purely rational evidence. Scientific knowledge requires no personal commitment. Galileo could well recant before the Inquisition. His retracting the hypothesis that the earth moves in no

[12] See Henri Poincaré, *Science et méthode* (Paris, 1908).

way affected the truth which soon gained universal validity. Following his trial, he is reputed to have said, "But it moves nevertheless." That scientific findings can be verified by anyone makes science an outstanding demonstration of clarity which must give assurance to the mind. This assurance will prevail in spite of the fact that what is universally accepted at a particular time will not necessarily always be considered valid. However, every scientific result, short-lived as its universal acceptance may be, is a step toward the final truth. It will give us the satisfaction of having achieved what our means enabled us to. While scientific discoveries often are of a temporary nature, they form bases of clarity upon which we can build a clearer, better world. *Die klare Welt bleibt klare Welt, im Auge nur ist's schlecht bestellt* (Goethe). Science means a perpetual striving to arrive and continuous arrival.

It will be argued that what has been said applies mainly to the natural sciences, to science in the English sense of the term, but not to *Wissenschaft*. The general pursuit of knowledge, however, also can be undertaken in a scientific manner and is concomitant to the search after truth. As was shown, that search often will yield results which sooner or later will be no longer considered truths but mere knowledge. Even then, these results continue to serve the truth, if only because we know that they are not truths. Similarly, the pursuit of knowledge, undertaken to find the truth, is likely to yield truths. The inclusion of the natural sciences in *Wissenschaft* is indicated when, in the first scene of the drama, Faust enumerates what he studied of the natural sciences, the social sciences, and the humanities and deplores "that we cannot know." While knowledge and truth perhaps should not be identified, truth is as much the aim of *Wissenschaft* as of the natural sciences. A *Wissenschaft* disparaging truth would be a contradiction in terms, for it would defy the natural sciences—that is, the very components which have grown most conspicuously and whose research methods have increasingly influenced other component disciplines.

Even before the growth of the natural sciences, other disciplines were advanced scientifically. Their advance was based upon scientific assumptions, and they employed scientific methods. Their findings were arrived at rationally. It is true that these findings often were not universally accepted. Frequently based upon speculation, they were more difficult to verify than the findings of the natural sciences. This does not mean, however, that they defied verification forever and that they could not come as close, or even closer, to the truth than the findings in the natural sciences. Just as the result of a *dolus eventualis* might be more severe than that of a plain *dolus,* a *veritas eventualis* might well turn out to be closer to the truth than a temporarily accepted *veritas evidentissima.* The frustrated scholar in the humanities who for some time fails to have his ideas universally accepted in the end may well be rewarded for his efforts and find that he has come closer to the truth than many a celebrated natural scientist.

As to the relationship between science and philosophy, Jaspers correctly finds close ties between the two. One cannot exist without the other. Philosophy motivates the will to know. It furnishes the ideas from which the scientist derives his vision, the ideas which determine his choices. In turn, philosophy acknowledges its bond to science. It does not permit itself to ignore realities. It demands to know what is cogent. Those who philosophize are impelled toward the sciences and seek experience in scientific methods.[13] Since the attitude of the scientist guarantees truthfulness, philosophers as lovers of the truth must be as interested in the protection of science as scientists as pursuers of the truth must be interested in philosophy. In a way, the true scientist is a philosopher and the true philosopher, a scientist. Since, like the scientist, the philosopher serves the truth, he belongs to the University as much as the scientist. Like the scientist, he contributes toward making the University a haven for clarity.

Home of the search for truth, the University has been a haven of clarity throughout history. Its very beginnings in the middle of the twelfth century mark it as a clarifying force. It emerged as an antidote to the turbulence of the investiture controversy. The quest for studies came about in a world which was torn by a dogmatic struggle between emperor and pope. About a hundred years later, *studium* had become firmly established next to *sacerdotium* and *imperium.* Its legitimacy was considered as valid as that of the pope and the emperor. The concept of historical translation was applied to studies as much as to the papacy and the empire. Just as, according to the Letter to the Hebrews, priesthood was transferred from the Old to the New Testament and from Jerusalem to Rome, and just as emperorship was transferred from Troy to Rome and Germany, *studium* was transferred from Greece to Rome and then, by Charlemagne, to Paris. The University of Paris became the prototype of the University as a haven for the pursuit of studies.

Studium was supposed to complement *sacerdotium* and *imperium,* to be an equal in a trinity of powers expressing a trinity of virtues—the spiritual, the temporal, and the rational. The study of things divine

[13] Karl Jaspers, *The Idea of the University* (Boston, 1959), 25f.

41

and human, of theology and law, and of the reason behind them, was hoped to bind together the spiritual and temporal powers which were about to fall apart. It was to reconcile faith and temporal justice and to restore clarity to a world which had become confused through the investiture controversy. Furthermore, studying was to restore clarity not only to the relationship between pope and emperor but also within the church and the empire. The University as the main seat of studying stood out as a demonstration of clarity not only in the confusion of the investiture controversy but also in the confusions of the Interregnum and the Great Schism.

Furthermore, the University became a clarity factor from the middle ages to modern age. Just as the co-imperium provided by St. Augustine's two swords theory erupted in the investiture controversy, the new triune theory, rather than reconciling *sacerdotium* and *imperium* through *studium,* resulted in a challenge of the former by the latter. As it turned out, *studium* was not just a mediator between but became a competitor of the church and the empire. This was natural. While an ad hoc task of studying, such as the reconciliation of the spiritual and temporal realms, could be conceived in the specific historical situation of the investiture controversy, *studium,* due to its unlimited nature, was to emancipate itself from any limitation of scope. Meaning a never-ending search for the truth, studying was bound to question institutions which could, and often did, veil or restrict the truth. It was bound to challenge faith with reason in both the spiritual and temporal realms. It was bound to question church and state. Since the pursuit of studies was located mainly in the universities, the latter became an important power after the church and state, aiding both in their attempts toward rationalization and clarification and at the same time admonishing them to remain within the scope of their respective *ratio.* In *Reflections on History,* Burckhardt spoke of the three powers, the state, religion, and culture. As the central institution for studying, the University can be considered a formidable exponent of culture, constantly furthering and limiting the other two powers.

Plato's academy was closed on orders of Emperor Justinian. The School of Alexandria was destroyed by Kalif Omar. The University has survived so far. Since the twelfth century, its development has been continuous. This longevity may well be due to the fact that studying, implying rational inquiry and a constant quest for truth, is innately immune to dogma and shifts in power. Considered the child of the church and the empire and usually founded with papal sanction, universities originally were based upon Christian belief. This rule was not questioned by the fact that the "antichrist" Frederic II founded the University of Naples to aid the emperor against the pope, that the University of Heidelberg resulted from the Great Schism, or that the University of Wittenberg was established without papal sanction. Under Charles V, the University of Paris assumed the title "eldest daughter of the King." In due time, the universities admitted liberal and antichristian positions. They became places of tolerance and the free search for the truth. Humanism, the Renaissance, and the Enlightenment not only "secularized" but also liberalized the University. In the name of the free mind, the pursuit of knowledge strove for an "open" conception of truth.

Originally the child of the church and the state, the University outgrew both. Equipped with neither a powerful clerical nor temporal organization, the University stood for nothing but the power of reason. Yet reason conquered dogma and the sword. The Catholic church founded many universities for the furtherance of its dogma but was unable to withstand the power of reason which clarified and often challenged dogma. The precursors of the Reformation, Wyclif and Hus, were university men. Luther taught theology at a university when he nailed his theses to the church door at Wittenberg. In the nineteenth century, Cardinal Newman, discussing the scope and aim of a university, came out in favor of "knowledge which is its own end, . . . liberal knowledge, or a gentleman's knowledge, . . . Knowledge which I have especially called Philosophy or, in an extended sense of the word, Science." "Liberal Education," he stated, "makes not the Christian, not the Catholic, but the gentleman. It is well to be a gentleman, it is well to have a cultivated intellect, a delicate taste, a candid, equitable, dispassionate mind, a noble and courteous bearing in the conduct of life;—these are the connatural qualities of a large knowledge; they are the objects of a University." [14] To this day, Catholic and Protestant institutions of learning have tended toward liberalizing and rationalizing religious dogmas, thus bringing clarity into the world of faith.

The situation is similar with respect to the state. Emperor Frederic II may have founded the University of Naples to train men for the imperial service. Absolute kings may have founded universities in order to educate civil servants who would support their regimes. If universities worked toward these aims, they generally did so in order to contribute to the rational government of the state rather than to the pursuit of reason of state. As a matter of fact, for the sake of reason, universities would pursue policies that could challenge prevalent political systems. Whereas it appears open to doubt whether the Univer-

[14] Newman, *Idea of a University*, 98, 107.

sity, an ideal, can ever be absolutely realized, by the nineteenth century many universities approached that ideal. They had become strongholds for rational thinking, institutions in which man's knowledge was accumulated and handed down to new generations. Through an ever-growing revelation of the truth, they gave to the world an ever-increasing clarity.

Since the idea of the university was realized through a growing emancipation from faith, modern trends toward making universities representative of new faiths must be steps backward. A university reflecting the outlook prevalent in a state, the outlook of a government, of an establishment, is likely to lose its quality as a University unless the established order is permeated by an unequivocal recognition of the value of rational investigation and instruction.

Jefferson and Wilhelm von Humboldt could well conceive of a university in the service of a state which recognized the value of permitting citizens to think rationally, saw the rationale for its existence in the protection of rational pursuits, and was, to use an expression by Robert von Mohl, a *Verstandesstaat*—a state governed by reason, a state of reason. As that name implies, there is in such a state no conflict between reason and state. Jefferson saw this kind of state approached in the United States, whose founders checked irrational politics by applying principles of political science. Von Humboldt saw it approached in the Germany of Beethoven, Goethe, Hardenberg, Savigny, Schiller, and Stein. Both Jefferson and von Humboldt hoped that the "state of reason" would prevail in the future because it precluded conflict between reason and state.

The situation was to be different as soon as the *Verstandesstaat* was replaced by a *Weltanschauungsstaat* which, while it could rationalize its organization into an effective power structure, no longer considered the pursuit of reason its *raison d'être* but made individuals follow a *Weltanschauung*. Rationalized as the latter might be, such a state would not suffer the unrestrained existence of reason. Instead of subordinating the state to reason, it would subordinate reason to the state. The state of reason would give way to reason of state. In such a situation, universities either would lose their quality as universities or become estates in defense of reason in a state of antireason.

The experience of National Socialism demonstrated the possibility of both alternatives. Under that regime, the universities in many respects lost their quality as strongholds for the cultivation of reason. The exodus of scholars like Einstein, Kelsen, Röpke, and others aided in reducing the universities' academic standing. Hitler's program of *Gleichschaltung* and the surveillance of university administrators and professors through the Gestapo and student leaders further promoted the decline. Yet the universities probably remained the most rational of public institutions, matched perhaps only by the judiciary, which incurred Hitler's anger because the judges would not pass judgments according to the *gesunde Volksempfinden*—the "sound popular sentiment." Much as the brown fire, which burned all of Germany, may have injured the universities, it was unable to destroy them. As in the past, reason proved to be stronger than faith. A short semester at the University of Berlin made me aware that the neoclassic spirit of Wilhelm von Humboldt was not dead even in the Third Reich. The Freiburg School of Economics, the student revolt at Munich, and many other manifestations bear witness to the fact that even in a most oppressive *Weltanschauungsstaat,* universities guarded the idea of the university and remained harbors for rational pursuits. This is borne out again in our own day. Participants in international conferences are impressed by the fact that the delegates of universities in totalitarian nations often act in a way that indicates a relative immunity of their academic institutions to the irrational slogans of political life.

That the University is conducive to clarity because it cultivates reason is not altered by modern trends toward specialization and the "multiversity."

At first sight, such trends suggest confusion. As was shown, the aim of the University is to find the truth (singular!). This is what Fichte had in mind when he called the scholar the priest of the truth and what is meant by the mottoes of American universities: *veritas* (Harvard), *lux et veritas* (Yale), *veritas vos liberabit* (Johns Hopkins). People might argue that if it is the aim of the *Uni*versity to find the *one* truth, then a specialized school will only find a specific part, and a multiversity, specific parts, of that truth. Such parts must be mere part-truths or perhaps half-truths. It might be asserted that partial or half-truths must confuse men, that specialization and the multiversity must add to the turbulence of youth in our time.

While these arguments ought not to be dismissed lightly, they can be countered. Trends toward specialization probably are not conducive to a general education. They will be detrimental to the educational ideal of *paideia.* They will lead to an alienation of the individual by providing him with too narrow a *Weltbild* and will result in frustration and confusion. However, a genuine and comprehensive education perhaps is no longer possible. We may have to put up with specialization. And perhaps trends toward specialization are not even as bad as they appear. They hardly are detrimental to the pursuit of truth

45

and the achievement of clarity. In a way, they are even implied in the idea of the university. The University, it must always be remembered, is *universitas scientiarum*—the university of sciences (plural), the union of various disciplines. While one could think of exploring all disciplines together, one can also examine them separately without contradicting the idea of the university. If the latter method was possible when there were relatively few disciplines and when it still was possible to know them all, then it must recommend itself when the various disciplines on account of their growth in number and complexity no longer can be mastered together. The truths found through specialized investigation in the end may well do more for the discovery of the truth than attempts to master all disciplines at once. Accumulated, these truths form an impressive mass of evidence. They also can be made fruitful by interdisciplinary collaboration, which appears to be a modern possibility of demonstrating the unity of the sciences.

The viability of special research has been demonstrated in the history of the University. The *studium generale* originally was established as a general place of study for the whole province of a monastic order because the *studia particularia,* the local monastic schools, were considered insufficient. The universities originally cultivated general, as distinguished from special, studies. The deductive method prevailed. With the expansion of knowledge and academic disciplines, particular studies were emphasized, and the inductive method gained ground. Specialization resulted from the desire for scientific investigation.

Special studies seldom hurt general studies. Specialization goes back to an early age. Medieval Salerno specialized in medicine, and Bologna, in law. This did not prevent these schools from becoming full-fledged universities. Göttingen in large measure was founded in order to provide education for the public service. It soon had a Lichtenberg, a Gauss, and a Weber and became a good all-round university. In the twentieth century, it became the Mecca for mathematicians and physicists. Hilbert, Planck, Hahn, and Heisenberg taught there. The latter also became known for his philosophical writings. Another physicist, von Weizsäcker, now holds a chair in philosophy. As Planck said, universal science no longer stands at the beginning but at the end of specialized research. There is a new universal science in the making "which is continually oriented and perfected by particular sciences." [15] This verdict of a scientist is matched by the statement of the philosopher Alois Dempf, who feels that the process of

---

[15] *Sitzungsberichte der Preussischen Akademie der Wissenschaften, Philosophisch-Historische Klasse* (Berlin, 1932), liiif.

differentiation will automatically result in a unity of the sciences.[16] As a multiversity, the University has held on to its mission in a society that to a large extent has become a multi-society.

UNIVERSITY AND FREEDOM

The advancement of the truth was due not only to the advancement of reason but also to that of freedom. For a rational discovery of the truth is not possible without freedom. Freedom is the alter ego of truth and reason: it is their end as well as their prerequisite.

Whereas the truth makes us free, freedom also lets us know the truth. Freedom is rooted in the openness to truth, but it also aids the discovery of the truth. In maintaining this I do not want to contradict John 8:32. I merely distinguish freedom as a reward for knowing the truth from freedom as a condition for doing so.

Christ, thinking he knew the truth, could well say, "Ye shall know the Truth and the Truth shall make you free." For most mortals, however, the truth is not some finished product generously given to them, something that can be found along the road and picked up casually. Rather, it is to be discovered through an unending and laborious search. Perhaps the passage just quoted implies such a search. If Christ spoke these words, he may well have realized that reports on his teachings might blur the truth and that future generations would have to labor toward coming closer to it. Perhaps his statement, connected as it is with men's struggle against sin, was meant to be an imperative to begin with. Certainly the scientist knows that he does not know the truth and that he must struggle for it. He senses that without effort there will be no reward. Knowing that matter does not disappear, he also knows that nothing comes about without putting something into it. *Rien pour rien. Ohne Fleiss kein Preiss.* If the reward for knowing the truth is freedom, he will expect to have to pay in kind and use his freedom for the discovery of the truth.

It is important to realize that only the freedom of the individual can aid in the discovery of the truth. Even among those who believe that truth is a sleeping beauty that was kissed awake by the Son of God and Man for the salvation of the human race, many realize that men have since obscured the truth. Others reject the idea of revelation altogether. Yet, most people believe that there is such a thing as the truth. They are eager to know it, although their desire is directed toward an

[16] Alois Dempf, *Die Einheit der Wissenschaft* (Stuttgart, 1955), 51. See, however, Richard Schwarz, *Wissenschaft und Bildung* (Freiburg, 1957).

ideal that cannot easily be realized. If knowing the one and only truth carries comprehensive freedom as a reward, and if men can receive only what they give, then freedom can be earned only through the total use by the human race of its total freedom for the discovery of the truth. It is obvious that this aim cannot be achieved easily. The ideal can be approached only through *individual* effort. This follows from the very nature of the human race. Since that race is composed of individuals, its freedom is the sum of the liberties of the individuals. The freedom of humanity thus presupposes the liberties of the individuals who compose it. In using their liberties for the discovery of the truth, individuals aid the human race in becoming free.

The individual, then, in order to help emancipate the human community, must be free in the specific organizations of that community. Leaving the individual free to pursue the discovery of the truth is the price a community has to pay for the final reward of freedom for those who compose it and, in the last analysis, for the freedom of mankind. Within a given community, this implies that the government or any group must abstain from interfering with a climate which is indispensable for the progress of science, including not only the natural and the so-called "positive" sciences but also philosophy and theology. For a philosopher's search for the truth may prove to be as important as that of a positive scientist, and the search for God may well prove to have been a search for truth.

Whereas the freedom of philosophy is not more important than that of the so-called positive sciences, it may warrant a greater emphasis on account of its smaller immunity from restrictions. The "value-free-ness" of the positive sciences generally will not bring them into conflict with external powers. Moreover, that the findings of those sciences can be proved rather easily provides them with a certain immunity because interference appears peculiar or ridiculous. This was as evident in Hitler's attempt to create a "German" physics as it was in Stalin's emphasis upon a "Communist" natural science. On the other hand, philosophical thinking often will favor values which conflict with those of the existing powers. Moreover, philosophical thinking cannot easily be verified and is rather vulnerable to attack. Since a philosophical inquiry often will pass beyond objectivized thought, it will hardly be possible without a dialogue which is "open." Perhaps philosophical knowledge is advanced more through the confrontation of thoughts than knowledge in the positive sciences. From the clash of ideas light is born. The situation is similar in theological thinking which also requires a climate of freedom if it is not to degenerate into a soulless formalism that is a caricature of faith. This has been recognized not only by Protestant but also by Catholic leaders. As Leo XIII said in *Immortale Dei*, it is important "to watch with the greatest care lest anyone be compelled to embrace the Catholic Faith against his will, for as St. Augustine wisely remarks, man is able to believe only by full consent."

Important as freedom from external interference is for finding the truth, it is not sufficient. It provides for the environment necessary for the pursuit of the truth but does not secure that pursuit. It is the legal guarantee of the freedom to seek the truth but not a command to the moral will to make use of that freedom. It is a device for the scholar's security but not for the daring sacrifice which is a prerequisite for finding the truth. This sacrifice must be made by the individual. Without the individual's willingness to dare and sacrifice, external freedom will be meaningless. For that freedom implies nothing but an abstention by external powers from interference. To make sense, its basically negative character must be positivized by those who profit from it. Governmental passivity must be complemented by the individual's activity. Here lies an important difference between liberal rights in general and the particular liberal right of seeking the truth. The former rights protect but do not require specific actions. As a matter of fact, the protection of freedom of speech is perhaps as valuable in the absence of speech as in its presence, for freedom of speech often has spawned nonsense, insult, and obscenity. The situation is similar in the case of such liberal rights as freedom of assembly, religion, the right to carry arms, etc. On the other hand, the protection of the right to seek the truth is without value if the truth is not actually sought. The freedom to seek the truth implies the duty to seek the truth. Just as law is an "ethical minimum" only, external freedom to seek the truth provides for an "academic minimum" only. And just as the individual citizen is expected to maximize the ethical minimum by leading not only a law-abiding but a moral life, the academic citizen is expected to maximize the academic minimum into a maximum by complementing his legal, external freedom by a moral, internal freedom.

The latter can manifest itself in a variety of ways. Although external freedom establishes certain legal limitations, these limitations often are blurred. For instance, a university administration, perhaps under pressure from a state government or a board of trustees, while not openly opposing the work of a professor, may do so deviously. It will not dismiss him or reduce his salary, but it may hurt him by not raising his salary, a means which in our age of tenure and rises in the cost of living is a subtle but effective way of interfering with academic freedom. The professor must then do all he can to promote the practical, and not just theoretical, existence of freedom. He must denounce everything which in his opinion in any way interferes with the free pursuit of the truth. External freedom must be nourished continually by the individual's unwavering willingness to assert it vis-à-vis the powers that are: he must demonstrate his internal freedom by ruthlessly exposing and challenging those above him. If he cannot muster the courage to do so, he must assert his internal freedom by continuing his work irrespective of disadvantages.

The same applies to his relations with his peers. The scholar must refrain from ingratiating himself with the members of his profession. For the sake of truth, he must not be afraid of deviating from what is generally accepted by them. He must be willing to go far out in criticizing established ideas, even at the risk of being ridiculed and of becoming unpopular. This attitude may cost him offers from other institutions and bring him other disadvantages. All of this must not deter him from maintaining his internal freedom.

As the scientist demonstrates his internal freedom from the powers above and around him, he also must assert it against those under him. He must resist the temptation of becoming a "popularizer" if that in any way makes him swerve from, or slow down, his pursuit of the truth. He must refuse to give in to popular tastes, be they expressed by the people at large, or, as happens frequently, by his students. The scientist must be willing to sacrifice popularity for his beliefs. He must acclaim truth, not men. He must strive for the truth, not for popular acclaim. For instance, in an environment of chauvinism during a war, he must be as willing to advocate pacifism, as in a climate of pacifism he must be willing to favor war.[17] He must approve research for purposes of war as much as for purposes of peace, for the search after truth is independent of war and peace. Discoveries useful for war usually will prove to be useful in peace, and vice versa. Nobel's invention of dynamite proved to be as much of a blessing in times of peace as it proved destructive in war. Even where such blessings cannot be discovered immediately, and irrespective of whether they will ever exist, the scientist must always assert his inner freedom to search for the truth. Nobel prizes for peace are matched by those for the sciences, and the winners of the latter are not judged by the popularity of their discoveries.

Some of the inner obligations of the scholar were prescribed by Fichte: "He should be motivated and confess to be motivated, by the love of his profession and of science only, irrespective of his own, or others', interests. . . . I could not imagine a priest of science, who

---

[17] Cf. Weber, *Wissenschaft als Beruf,* 584f.

thinks of ordaining new priests of science, not saying what the latter do not like to hear because they do not like to hear it, in order that they may continue to listen to him. . . . Every word the academic teacher announces must reflect science and his eagerness to spread it. Every word must unveil his dearest love for his audience—not as his listeners, but as the future servants of science. Science and the living avidity to make it comprehensible, not the teacher, shall speak. Aspiring to talk in order to talk, to talk beautifully in order to talk beautifully so that others may know it; the mania for forming words and beautiful words, is undignified for any person if he does not say anything on the subject matter, especially for an academic teacher who represents the dignity of science to future generations." [18]

What Fichte called the priest of the truth, then, must have the inner courage to question. The scientist must have the internal freedom to "wonder why the universe should be as it is," to reduce "the actual to fluidity by breaking up its literal sequences in his imagination." [19] He must take a new look at the world and challenge existing knowledge for the promotion of the truth. The free scholar must "let being be." [20] He must leave reality and truth alone and contest everything that obscures reality and the truth.

The freedom to discover the truth makes the most sense if it is exercised rationally. Just as freedom is the end as well as the prerequisite for truth, it is the end as well as the prerequisite of reason.

Seeking the truth implies judgment. Just as the judge, confronted with facts and laws, renders a judgment and, by obeying the legal imperative, frees himself and his fellow men from legal dispute and uncertainty, so the scientist, faced by facts and laws, through his judgment fulfills his obligation to the scientific imperative and frees himself and his fellow men from scientific dispute and uncertainty. In distinction to the scientist, however, the judge may bring a *sacrificium intellectus*. Following Kant's statement that "a legal, although not very legitimate, constitution is better than none," [21] he judges in conformity with the laws, irrespective of whether he considers them just or not. In passing a verdict, he may pronounce a legal truth which by the standards of ultimate truth is an error. He may do so with a relatively good conscience, for he is not a lawmaker and his obedience to the existing, if unjust, law fulfills an important function of the law, namely,

[18] Johann Gottlieb Fichte, *Ueber das Wesen des Gelehrten, und seine Erscheinungen im Gebiete der Freiheit* (1805), *Sämmtliche Werke*, VI, 437.

[19] William James, *Psychology* (New York, 1892), 369.

[20] "Freiheit enthüllt sich jetzt als das Seinlassen von Seiendem . . . das Sicheinlassen auf das Seiende." Martin Heidegger, *Vom Wesen der Wahrheit* (Frankfurt, 1954), 14.

[21] Immanuel Kant, *Zum ewigen Frieden* (Königsberg, 1795), Appendix 1.

legal security. *Plutôt une injustice qu'un désordre.* The scientist cannot with a good conscience make an intellectual sacrifice. To begin with, there is no such thing as scientific security to justify such behavior. Science is insecure by definition and must remain so as long as the search for the truth continues—probably as long as science exists. The scientist must never make a judgment in order to conform to accepted laws. It is true that his judgments, like those of a judge, often will be based on existing laws, but whereas the judge must conform to the laws, the scientist must not. He must challenge them if he considers them wrong and untenable. He must render his judgment not in conformity with what men have said the law of science to be but according to his own investigations of the truth. Unlike a judge, a scientist is not always bound by the facts and the laws that rule them. He discovers new facts and new laws. In rendering judgment, the judge obeys the human legislator; the scientist can be "legislator." A judge obeys what men think they have discovered of the laws of nature and of God. A scientist discovers the laws of nature and the creations of God. A judge is bound by the work of men. A scientist is bound only by the work of God. For the judge, the principle *non sub homine sed sub deo et lege* is an ideal, but it is a reality for the scientist.

True judgment is rational judgment. Indeed, judgment could be called applied reason. If freedom therefore is the reward for judgment, freedom also must be the reward for reasoning. Furthermore, freedom is a prerequisite for reasoning, or active reason: there can be no fair judgment without the freedom to reason.

It has been generally accepted, from the ancient Greeks through the Middle Ages down to our time, that the power of self-determination is an attribute of reason and that without reason there can be no freedom. Perhaps the decline of freedom in our century is due to the fact that freedom has become detached from reason. More and more people feel they can do without rational reflection and live, as Heidegger put it, as "anonymous somebodies" on the level of "the daily chatter," be they influenced by Marx who considered freedom the result of technical progress, by Nietzsche who defined freedom as the will to power, by Gide who called freedom a gratuitous act, or by Sartre who felt that freedom was a choice which is nothing but pure invention.[22] Freedom presupposes choice, and choice implies reasoning. Freedom without reason does not make much sense. The more rational a decision or judgment is, the freer it is. The mathematician Spinoza was a natural advocate of academic freedom, for mathematical judgments,

[22] See Albert Dondeyne, "Truth and Freedom: A Philosophical Study," in Louis de Raeymaeker et al., *Truth and Freedom* (Louvain, 1955), 39.

reflecting a maximum of rationality, enjoy a maximum of freedom. Only a fool will challenge them.

Just as freedom does not seem to be possible without reason, reason does not seem to be possible without freedom. Whereas reason makes us free, freedom permits us to reason. Even St. Thomas, who emphasized that reason is the ultimate foundation of freedom, spoke of a *liberum judicium,* a free judgment as distinguished from a judgment that makes free.[23] As reason generates freedom, freedom activates reason into reasoning. Freedom provides reason with a rationale and gives sense to reason. Freedom enables reason to be reason-able.

As to the various aspects of the freedom to reason, the remarks made in connection with the freedom to discover the truth basically apply. This is not surprising in view of the close relationship between reason and the truth. While the two are not identical—all too often the truth is reasoned away—they are in a large measure interdependent and come close to being alter egos. The truth is mainly discovered by reason and is reasonable.

There are, then, external and internal freedoms of reasoning. The former guarantees a minimum of the freedom to reason from interference by outside powers; the latter implies the assertion and maximization of that minimum. The external freedom of reasoning involves legal guarantees upon which the individual can base claims. The internal freedom involves a moral duty to stand up and bring sacrifices for the freedom of reasoning. Making the most of one's internal freedom appears to be a fair compensation for profiting from external freedom. Having originally obliged external powers to recognize external freedom, internal freedom now obliges the individual to show himself worthy of external freedom. While profiting from external freedom will be easy, living up to the moral requirements of internal freedom will often be an arduous task. That task cannot be achieved by the many Papagenos that populate this world but only by the few Taminos who will be rewarded admission to the temple of wisdom.

The freedoms to reason and to seek the truth are the basic ingredients of academic freedom. Academic freedom thus is more than merely the right to pursue research and teaching. It implies the obligation to promote learning. Aside from pursuing his own learning, the individual must promote learning in an absolute sense. He must protect everything conducive to learning and fight everything detrimental to it. If learning is promoted by the government, then the government ought to be supported. If learning is promoted by professors and stu-

---

[23] St. Thomas Aquinas, *Summa Theologica,* p. I, qu. 83, a.1 and a.3 *ad* 2.

dents, they ought to be supported. If learning is prevented by the government, the government must be fought. If learning is prevented by professors or students, then they must be fought. Academic freedom must be blind to status.

The individual will not always be confronted with simple alternatives which make a choice easy. Often the situation will be blurred. He will be faced with difficult choices which will be true tests of his readiness to stand up for academic freedom. For instance, he must risk being called illiberal and denounce academic license. For academic license is a perversion of academic freedom and can be as detrimental to learning as external oppression. Since such license often will appear in the disguise of internal academic freedom and denounce the existing external academic freedom, the individual, unaware of the disguise, will think he is faced with an option between the former and the latter. He will tend to favor the former, thinking that internal freedom probably brought about external freedom to begin with, that the former is supposed to nourish and expand the latter, that it reflects a moral maximum rather than a legal minimum. While these thoughts deserve consideration, they may not warrant preferring internal over external academic freedom. Whereas the former can come close to a maximum, it will only be a vague moral maximum—something unsafe. On the other hand, while external freedom generally will only constitute a minimum, it is a concrete legal minimum—something safe. It probably is better to have this safe minimum which can be maximized than the unsafe maximum which, being without legal sanction, can all too easily be minimized out of existence. While in the presence of external freedom, internal freedom can yield enormous results; in its absence, it might not amount to anything.

Academic freedom is not license. Its practical existence presupposes a legal order. While it is conceivable to have freedom without such an order, the world has not yet reached this stage. Legal orders are the main guarantors of freedom, including academic freedom. Their governments must maintain academic freedom against anything that jeopardizes the progress of learning, irrespective of whether it derives from the government, from the public, from faculty, or from students. Governments thus may have a role in putting down riots, something universities often will be unable to do. Whether governments also should have a part in the promotion and hiring of faculty is another question. There can be no doubt that in that respect the self-administration of universities has disadvantages. "Fear of outside competition and of excellence tends to turn self-administrative bodies into monopolistic cliques interested in safeguarding their own mediocrity. Inevitably, the promotion and hiring pattern will then reflect a gradual and almost imperceptible lowering of standards. The system of co-option by itself will fail to produce ever better men and will instead favor a mediocre common denominator." [24] While this danger can be reduced by taking hiring and promoting out of the jurisdiction of the respective departments and by assigning it to interdepartmental committees, a power outside the university might be preferable. Still, government activity in the hiring and promotion of faculty is risky. It might introduce politics into the universities and be detrimental to academic freedom.

Similar considerations apply to private universities. These institutions are legal communities of administrators, employees, and students, implying academic freedom and the obligation not to interfere with learning. Although academic freedom is blind to the status of the members of an academic community, its defenders cannot afford to be blind to the fact that the university government gives sanction to the university order and is the protector of academic freedom. This government—usually the administration and tenured faculty—has the duty to protect that freedom. The members of a university government who fail to put academic license in its place, who fail to maintain the regular process of learning, forfeit their place in the university as much as those who threaten academic freedom by interfering with learning through license and violence.

The history of academic freedom has been most obvious with respect to the freedom from external interference, and the universities played a major role in securing that freedom. This role was already evident in the Middle Ages when the universities were under the control of the church. In 1229, the University of Toulouse invited teachers, promising them the liberty to study Aristotle. John Wyclif was backed by Oxford University in his early opposition to the church. After John Hus had been condemned by the Council of Constance, the University of Prague tried to save him. When, early in the sixteenth century, Pietro Pomponazzi denied that the immortality of the soul could be proven by Aristotelian methods and risked persecution by opposing church dogma and the clergy, Italian universities clamored for his services. The University of Bologna raised his salary in order to keep him. When Luther posted his 95 theses, he was backed by the University of Wittenberg. Giordano Bruno perhaps lived as long as he did only because he was sheltered by northern universities. In 1588, he thanked the University of Wittenberg for having permitted him the liberty of philosophical research. A little earlier, the Uni-

[24] Jaspers, *Idea of the University*, 127.

versity of Leiden was founded to reflect the liberalism and cosmopolitanism of the Netherland towns and to follow a policy of academic freedom. Professors were not required to make doctrinal commitments in their simple loyalty oath to the university and the city; Jews were admitted; a Catholic professor whom Protestants in town had driven to resign because he defended religious persecution was asked by the university to return.

Following the publication of treatises favoring academic freedom—notably Bacon's *Prometheus* (1609) and *New Atlantis* (1627) and Milton's *Areopagitica* (1644)—universities intensified the promotion of that freedom. In 1673, Spinoza was invited to Heidelberg with the assurance that he would be given "the most ample liberty to philosophize," provided this liberty would not be "abused to disturb the religion publicly established." He declined the invitation largely on account of the latter proviso. Before the century was over, in 1694, the University of Halle was founded with a view to rejecting the principle *cuius regio, eius universitas*. Although that university had to labor to remain independent of Pietist and royal influences, as was evident in the dismissal of Christian Wolff, a staunch advocate of academic freedom, its courageous faculty attacked the Aristotelian concept of science based on deductions from principles. A new concept of science, based upon observation, experience, experiment, and mathematical equations, came into being. Research was put on a par with teaching. New disciplines were discovered. Laboratories, institutes, clinics, and seminars were introduced. In this process of change, the University of Göttingen, founded in 1737 to promote academic freedom, played a major role. One hundred years later, seven of its professors (the famous *Göttinger Sieben*), led by the liberal F. C. Dahlmann and including the brothers Grimm, stood up for freedom under the constitution. Their dismissal by the king in 1837 outraged liberals throughout Germany. As a result, the National Assembly of Frankfurt, counting among its members most of the dismissed professors, provided in section 152 of its draft for a German constitution that "science and its teaching are free." The same text can be found in section 20 of the Prussian constitution of 1850. These provisions reflect the ideal of the University of Berlin, established in 1809. Its founders stressed that, aside from the self-administration of the university and its right to adjudicate matters within its jurisdiction, academic freedom implied the individualistic principle of free creative learning and teaching. Wilhelm von Humboldt had been the author of *Ideas to an Attempt to Determine the Limits of State Activity*, a study which attacked enlightened absolutism. Favoring "total individuality", he felt

56

that this aim could best be achieved in a university which served the "pure idea of science." [25] Academic freedom had reached a dimension to which not much could be added.

UNIVERSITY AND COMMUNITY

The individualistic nature of academic freedom makes its existence in authoritarian communities tenuous. This has been obvious throughout its history, showing oppressions by the rulers of church and state, claims to academic freedom by individuals and universities, and the final guarantee of that freedom by the authorities. While up to the nineteenth century academic freedom increased, the twentieth century has witnessed growing infringements by totalitarian regimes.

This is not surprising. Whereas it is conceivable that at some future date the truth will have been discovered and be represented by a totalitarian government, our civilization has not yet reached that stage. No existing regime can claim to represent the truth. Governments making such a claim must be telling a lie. Consequently, they must be afraid of and opposed to a freedom which is to expose the lie. If totalitarians would admit that they are opposed to the truth, the discussion could end. Such an admission is improbable however, because it would call their legitimacy into question. Hitler's statement, "The bigger the lie the better," while it was an ominous forecast of things to come, expressed a political design to come to power rather than an admission that his regime would be one of the big lie. Totalitarian regimes maintain that they represent the truth and pay homage to their version of the truth, acting as their own judges.

Naturally, totalitarians must be afraid of the scientists, the priests of the truth, and must fight academic freedom. Academic freedom, being the freedom to discover the truth, presupposes that the truth has not been discovered. It must contest the "truths" or ideologies of existing regimes and provoke these regimes to counter-measures. Modern totalitarian regimes, under which *Weltanschauungen* have become new state religions, extended the principle of the peace of Augsburg, *cuius regio, eius religio,* into the principle, *cuius regio, eius universitas.* As institutions pursuing the rational search after truth, universities came under attack. Whereas they became separate islands in which scien-

---

[25] Cf. his "Über die innere und äussere Organisation der höheren wissenschaftlichen Anstalten in Berlin" (1810?), *Wilhelm von Humboldts Gesammelte Schriften,* ed. Preussische Akademie der Wissenschaften (Berlin, 1903–36), X, 250ff.

tists retained a greater degree of autonomy than ordinary citizens, they became politicized at the cost of academic freedom.

This was evident under the Hitler regime which made plain that its ideology in large measure was based upon belief. It is evident in to-day's totalitarian nations. Stalin is reputed to have said: "We are confronted by a fortress. The name of this fortress is science with its innumerable branches. Youth must take this fortress, if it wishes to build a new life, if it wishes to replace the old guard." [26] He undermined the universities by stressing the scientific character of communism. While the communist regime made certain concessions to academic freedom, it still emphasized that "discussion of any scientific problem should be based above all on the Leninist principle of the party nature of science and scholarship, and participants in a discussion must approach the solution of all disputes from a position of Marxist-Leninist methodology, the only scientific basis for cognition of the objective world. Fruitful discussion can be based only on the Marxist outlook." [27]

On reading this, one tends to agree that "no state intolerant of any restriction on its power for fear of the consequences of a pure search for truth, will ever allow a genuine university to exist." [28] In other words, "the university is unassimilable, because of its function, a function of profound significance for the political order: the search for truth. Those who are dedicated to it, and to the extent that they are, will of necessity withdraw from the battle cries of the market place into the quiet laboratory and library, there to reexamine the assumptions upon which the actions of rulers and their helpers are based." [29] In totalitarian regimes, the general absence of external academic freedom must be made up by an extra assertion of internal academic freedom. While oppression is as little the father of all things as war, it is perhaps in the face of oppression that an unwavering loyalty to the truth can best be proved. Perhaps only under conditions of hardship can the individual show his willingness to bring sacrifices to the truth. Perhaps only then can the scientist prove his courage to make material sacrifices in order not to make intellectual sacrifices. Perhaps only then can he demonstrate that for the truth he would jeopardize not only his earnings but also his physical liberty—and even his life. Perhaps only then can he illustrate his determination to be the martyr

[26] Quoted in Carl J. Friedrich, *Man and his Government* (New York, 1963), 633.
[27] "Journalists' Review: On Discussions in Scientific Journals," *Kommunist* (May, 1955), 119.
[28] Jaspers, *Idea of the University*, 121.
[29] Friedrich, *Man and his Government*, 633.

Nietzsche hoped he would be as a servant of *humanitas*. Perhaps only in the face of adversity can the scholar become a saint.

What has been said about the position of the University in totalitarian communities is relevant to its position in democratic communities. That Western democracies acknowledge academic freedom should not blind us to the possibility that democratic communities can hurt the University. This is evident in the case of democratic totalitarianism. Because its function is to search for truth, the University must be "unassimilable," not only in the totalitarian dictatorships described but in any kind of dictatorship, including that of the majority. Whereas I am reluctant to agree with Hitler and Stalin that their regimes were more democratic than Western counterparts, it is not unlikely that both men generally executed the will of the majority. Since there is no basic difference between the oppression potential of the majorities that supported Hitler and Stalin and majorities that exist in Western democracies (the latter are, in view of the constant support for certain types of legislation, not as "temporary" as is often believed), majority rule in Western democracies can be ideological and oppressive. Consequently, a university "committed" to totalitarian democracy must be as dubious as one committed to other forms of totalitarianism, especially if its commitment implies a reluctance to question democratic tenets. The University cannot be committed to refrain from questioning, for questioning is indispensable to its function. Just as the idea of the university was realized by questioning dogmas such as "the voice of the church is the voice of God" and "the voice of the king is the voice of God," it must now be realized by questioning the dogma that the voice of the people is the voice of God.

The evil of democratic despotism must not let us ignore the potential evil of constitutional democracy, small though it may be. The tension between constitutional democracy and universities seldom is evident. It usually is subtle. But it is this very lack of evidence, this very subtlety, that requires us to be on our guard. What constitutional democracy might be unable, or not want, to achieve through the force of law, it might try to bring about through moral pressure. The "phantom public" might attempt to prevail upon the University. The University must resist such pressures, camouflaged and inveigling as they may be. It must be as "unassimilable" in a free society as in an unfree one. The University's sole commitment must be to the truth.

The obligation of the University not to be committed ideologically is stronger under free governments than under authoritarian ones because the former generally guarantee a greater degree of academic freedom, which puts greater obligations upon those enjoying it. The "commitment" of the University under totalitarian regimes can be compared to a mutilation, even a murder, of the University by the public power. The University is a victim, although often an innocent victim. Under a free government, an ideological commitment of the University by those who run it is less excusable. It is like self-mutilation or suicide. In the former case, academic freedom is trampled upon by the authorities outside the University; in the latter, it is disregarded and abused by the members of the University themselves. Academic citizens commit the most sinful of academic sins when, instead of complementing external academic freedom by a vigorous assertion of internal academic freedom, they neglect the latter and make the former meaningless. The moral responsibility of scholars and scientists is greater under free governments than under authoritarian ones. When scholars and scientists refrain from asserting academic freedom in the face of governmental oppression, they only miss becoming saints. When they voluntarily render academic freedom meaningless, they become traitors.

It follows that the emphases these days upon the University's obligation to "public service" and "community service" is detrimental to the idea of the university unless such service promotes the rational exploration of the truth. The University is neither a trade school nor a community center. To the degree that a university becomes a "community school," it loses its quality as a university. The disastrous results of "committing" a university to public service are evident in the Free University of Berlin and in Columbia University.

The Free University was founded as an antithesis to the unfree university in East Berlin. Unfortunately, its founders went beyond establishing a university for the sake of freedom. Attributing the absence of academic freedom in the University of East Berlin to the absence of democracy under the Ulbricht regime, they believed that democracy was a prerequisite for, and perhaps the only guarantee of, freedom. They committed the new university not merely to freedom but to democratic freedom. In contrast to Wilhelm von Humboldt, for whom freedom meant the freedom to doubt everything, they believed that democracy was beyond doubt. This belief was reflected in the constituent act in which students, faculty, and the government of Berlin participated. It was reflected in the university's charter which provided for the government of the university by students and faculty. However, a free university serving democracy is a contradiction in terms unless democracy is unequivocally committed to the exploration of the truth. While democracy may serve the truth better than other forms of government, it is not doing so by definition. Aside from being harmful to the truth, democracy also can be detrimental to freedom, especially if it degenerates into absolute democracy. Soon, the Free University's commitment to democracy became its undoing. The parity among *veritas, libertas,* and *justitia,* indicated on the university's coat of arms, became shaken beyond the intentions of even the most democratic of its founders. Democratic justice came to overshadow truth and liberty. Not surprising in view of the fact that social democrats had been predominant in the founding of the Free University, the left-wingers within the university became stronger and stronger. Organized in groups such as "Communes" and the Socialist German Student League (SDS), they attempted to further democratize the Free University, to engage it increasingly in the service of social democracy, and to make it more community-conscious. Their plans made one wonder whether they wanted to communize the university in spite of their denunciations of the Communist regimes in East Germany and Russia. Carrying red flags, they used terror and violence and truncated the Free University.

Terror and violence under red flags also mutilated Columbia University. While not founded with the idea of serving democracy, that university became the victim of the democratic trend toward social democracy, of attempts to make it serve the community. The rioters put their community-consciousness above the idea of the university. They blamed Columbia for promoting research and analysis relating to national defense and domestic riot control. In their opinion, such research was detrimental to a world community without imperialism, a community desired by themselves and by antiwar demonstrators. Specifically, they attacked Columbia's plan to build a gymnasium in a park located between the university and Harlem, maintaining that the university was encroaching on the negro community, although the park belonged as little to Harlem as it did to Columbia, the gymnasium was to occupy only two out of the park's thirty acres, and the land for the construction of the gymnasium had been leased to the university by the City of New York.

University commitment to community beliefs is a disservice not only to the University but also to the community. Since today no world, national, state, or local community knows the whole truth, subordination of the University to any community must delay the enlightenment of the community and the blessings that come with it. It must be kept in mind that the best service to the community is the furtherance of the truth—not that what according to public opinion is good for the community is necessarily true but that only what is true

61

is necessarily good for the community. What people think is good for the community must not be the guiding principle of the University, for only respect for the immanently guiding principle of the University—the search for the truth—can be good for the people.

In view of the basic differences between modern universities and democracies, making universities serve the wishes of democratic communities must mean subordinating an educated, liberty-promoting elite to less educated, equality-possessed common men and denying the latter education and emancipation. It amounts to subordinating trends toward order to trends toward anarchy, to depriving communities of stabilizing factors. It means subordinating institutions in which reason prevails to the masses in which emotions run higher and depriving the masses of a chance to become more reasonable. It amounts to subordinating clarity to confusion and to depriving communities of the light that could let them see the truth and move into clarity.

A University serves a community best if it refrains from catering to the temporary wishes of men and instead aids the long-range aim of humanity to make humans humane by showing them the way to truth. Born of the humane quest for the truth, the University's mission is to serve humanity through the pursuit of the truth. Since that pursuit is a matter of the human brain, it can be undertaken by individuals only. Consequently, the best service the University can render to the community is to emphasize the freedom of the individual to search for the truth irrespective of community desires. Against the self-contradictory democratic triune, *liberté, égalité, fraternité,* a triune which resulted in the increasing deterioration of liberty, I would pit, as an antidote to the mysticism that surrounds the number four with most primitive communities, the clear scientific quaternion, *universitas, libertas, veritas, humanitas.*

3

YOUTH IN UNIVERSITY
From Confusion to Clarity

YOUTHFUL UNIVERSITY

The suggestion that for the sake of truth and clarity, the University is not to be committed to community service, raises the question of the University's attitude toward youth. If the University is "closed" to the desires of the community, must it not also be closed to the desires of youth? Quite to the contrary.

When I opposed a University commitment to the community, I had in mind a closed community committed to certain beliefs, certain ways, and specific plans conducive to the community's convenience— a community that could impose its will upon, or at least influence, the University, to the detriment of the exploration of the truth. Specifically, this community was political, whether on a local, state, national, or world level. To this closed community I opposed a University closed to the political desires of the community in order to remain open to the exploration of the truth.

The situation is different with respect to the community of youth. Although youth has appeared as a community, it is doubtful whether it really constitutes a community. It certainly is not a political community. It does not possess a government that could execute its will. A large percentage of youth cannot vote. Whereas this percentage can influence voters, its influence, even if combined with that of the voting members of youth, will be minor. There are other indications that youth cannot influence the University to neglect its mission. Youth not only is devoid of government but also of "set" values. No matter how much one hears about the values of youth, they are not as set as the values of adults are. Much as a political community may be divided up into parties and factions, there generally will exist a certain consensus in its government. Even governments based on often shifting coalitions demonstrate that consensus. One need think only of France under the Third and Fourth Republics, or of the Weimar Republic. On the other hand, one cannot speak of a consensus of youth. Always looking for its identity, youth is torn between values between which it constantly shifts back and forth. Mature realism, the realization that there are many things in the world one had better put up with, makes the older set in their ways. Immature idealism, the disgust about many things that surround youth, and the hope that the world can be improved, make the young worrying firebrands. The old are resigned to many lies. The young are eager to make truth prevail.

These considerations show that the University's attitude toward youth can be different from its attitude toward adult communities. While the University can be annoyed by the fads of youth, youth constitutes less danger for the University than the government of the adult community. The latter can legally abolish a university. Youth only can give a university a hard time—and that at the risk of being thrown out of the university and into jail. Even if we take the protection of the University from external interference for granted, the University risks less by serving youth than by serving the political community. It is risky to serve those one may become subservient to. Since there is a good chance that the University may become subservient to the political community, it must be wary of serving that community. As long as there is no danger of the University's becoming subservient to youth, it can afford serving them. Furthermore, serving youth is unlikely to jeopardize the University because its basic mission to explore the truth is similar to the basic desire of youth to know the truth. The "openness" of youth to truth can be matched by the University's "openness" to serve youth.

The University is well suited to serve youth, for as a servant of science it is an innately youthful institution. Science is but the other side of youth. It is youth predominantly rational and implies constant rejuvenation. Concluding his essay, "The Organization of Thought," Whitehead, speaking of natural science, stated: "We may conceive humanity as engaged in an internecine conflict between youth and age. Youth is not defined by years but by the creative impulse to make something. The aged are those who, before all things, desire not to make a mistake. Logic is the olive branch from the old to the young, the wand which in the hands of youth has the magic property of creating science." [1]

This statement is valid not only for the natural sciences but for science in general. Science is *Wissenschaft,* not *Wissensbesitz,* for *Wissenschaft* is not what *Wissen geschafft* but what *Wissen schafft.* It is not

[1] Alfred N. Whitehead, *The Aims of Education and Other Essays* (New York, 1957), 179.

the knowledge accumulated by virtue of previous knowledge but the exploration of the truth through the broadening and questioning of existing knowledge. Accumulated knowledge is a prerequisite to modern science, but it is not science itself. It owes its existence to the scientific process, to the constant challenge to existing beliefs and the constant arrival at new truths. Our knowledge has come about through "the creative impulse to make something"—through youth, through science. More and more must be made out of it through scientific rejuvenation. *Wissensbesitz* owes its existence to, and must be enlarged by, *Wissenschaft*. As in the past, the scientific process must continue and with it, the creative impulse that basically is an attribute of youth. Whitehead is right in emphasizing that it is important for science that men show youthful behavior by not being afraid of making mistakes.

Since I am concerned with science in general and not just with natural science, I might add that logic alone cannot be the wand that has the *magic* property of creating science. Only logic combined with speculation can perform that task. Even illogical speculation could advance science, if only by accident; as long as that chance exists, illogical speculation ought not to be precluded. Otherwise one runs the risk of fearing to make mistakes.

Our previous remarks on public opinion versus the University and Whitehead's comments on age and youth bring to mind some of John Stuart Mill's ideas. The great liberal distinguished set "popular opinions" from "heretical opinions." The former "are often true, but seldom or never the whole truth" and are "exaggerated, distorted, and disjointed from the truths by which they ought to be accompanied and limited" but which they suppress and neglect instead. The latter "are generally some of these suppressed and neglected truths, bursting the bonds which kept them down, and either seeking reconciliation with the truth contained in the common opinion, or fronting it as enemies." Mill made plain that "every opinion which embodies somewhat of the portion of truth which the common opinion omits, ought to be considered precious, with whatever amount of error and confusion that truth may be blended."

What Mill applied to the freedom of all men, applies *a fortiori* to men in universities: "First, if any opinion is compelled to silence, that opinion may, for aught we can certainly know, be true. To deny this is to assume our own infallibility. Second, though the silenced opinion be an error, it may, and very commonly does, contain a portion of the truth; and since the general or prevailing opinion on any subject is rarely or never the whole truth, it is only by the collision of adverse opinions that the remainder of the truth has any chance of being supplied. Third, even if the received opinion be not only true, but the whole truth, unless it is suffered to be, and actually is, vigorously and earnestly contested, it will, by most of those who receive it, be held in the manner of a prejudice, with little comprehension or feeling of its rational grounds. And not only this, but, fourthly, the meaning of the doctrine itself will be in danger of being lost, or enfeebled, and deprived of its vital effect on the character and conduct; the dogma becoming a mere formal profession, inefficacious for good, but cumbering the ground, and preventing the growth of any real and heartfelt conviction, from reason or personal experience." [2]

Whitehead was aware not only of the youthfulness of science but also of the youthfulness of the University. In "Universities and their Function," he envisaged universities as "homes of adventures" in which those advanced in years would share with their juniors the wonders of exploration. "For successful education there must always be a certain freshness in the knowledge dealt with. It must either be new in itself or it must be invested with some novelty of application to the new world of new times. Knowledge does not keep any better than fish. You may be dealing with knowledge of the old species, with some old truth; but somehow or other it must come to the students, as it were, just drawn out of the sea and with the freshness of its immediate importance." [3] What he had in mind has been a distinctive feature of the University. If youth is not defined by years but by the creative impulse to make something, then youth is the very essence of the University. There is hardly another institution where those advanced in years are as committed to the desire of exploring new frontiers as their younger colleagues, where discovering new land is the very rationale for everyone's existence.

Schumpeter called the academic man a revolutionary by profession. There is something to that, even though the expression is not happily chosen. As far as the advancement of learning is concerned, universities have been innovating in a constant evolution, characterized by never-ending attempts of those young in mind to explore the truth and to expand knowledge. In view of this evolution, the *universitas scientiarum* always has been the kind of youthful institution desired by the neo-humanist Fichte. After an exhortation that scholars as the servants of science always must advance learning, Fichte emphasized the youthfulness of the scholar's work. Science, he said, must always,

---

[2] John Stuart Mill, *On Liberty and Considerations on Representative Government,* ed. R. B. McCallum (Oxford, 1946), 40f., 46f.

[3] Whitehead, *Aims of Education,* 147.

again and again, blossom in the scholar. "He must remain in this condition of fresh intellectual youth. Nothing must become rigid or petrified for him. Every sunrise should bring a new enterprising love for his work and new opinions." For the scholar, "the fountain of youth must flow. To this fountain he must faithfully surrender himself as long as it carries him." [4]

YOUTH AS A COMMUNITY OF SCHOLARS

The University is a youthful institution, not merely on account of the youthful character of science and the latter's servants, but also on account of the physical youth of most of the members of its community. These members are the students, who are generally from about 18 to 26 years of age. In distinction to the students of a high school, *Gymnasium,* or *lycée,* university students belong rather exclusively to the age group of youth. There probably is no other free and civil institution in which youthful membership would be so normal, which would be so youthful by definition, which would be as likely to be left by its members as they grow older. The armed forces have a regular turnover of young men, but they are neither a free, nor a civil, institution. The percentage of youthful members in athletic clubs is usually not as high as it is in universities. As to youth organizations, the age of their members usually is comparable to that of high school students.

There is probably no other place in which the outside world would be as much aware of youth as the environment of a University. We are all too much aware of this today, when headlines on youth generally are headlines relating to the universities. Youth, however, has also put its mark on communities in which universities are located in normal, quieter times. Although (or because?) he never studied in a university, Mark Twain wittily described foreign student life in *A Tramp Abroad.* The situation has not changed much to this day. The story that every new student arriving at a small university is formally received by university dignitaries as a cherished rarity is, of course, exaggerated. Still, students influence, and often determine, life in university towns and give to these towns a youthful appearance. Whether the visitor sees a student parade or a football game in America, or whether he comes across European students in their picturesque fraternity uniforms, he is taken in by the youthfulness of a university

[4] Fichte, *Über die Bestimmung des Gelehrten,* 329; *Ueber das Wesen des Gelehrten,* 438.

town. This youthfulness prompts all too many graduates to make university towns their home, with the result that they become crowded with professional people who often can scarcely make a living.

Those who leave upon graduation often leave with a heavy heart and the sad feeling that their youth is over. To them, a longing for youth often becomes identified with a longing for their student days, beautifully expressed in the Academic Festival Overture by Brahms, who, like Mark Twain, never studied in a University nor for that matter in a conservatory. At the beginning of his autobiography, the aged Jefferson credited the College of William and Mary with having provided him "the great good fortune, and what probably fixed the destinies of my life," of meeting two teachers. The destinies of their lives were fixed in the youthful atmosphere of universities for the Brownings, the John Stuart Mills, the Schellings, and many others who met there and married. As is evident in his first lecture *On the Future of Our Institutions of Learning,* Nietzsche's memories of youth in a large measure were those of his student days. The same is true of thousands of less well-known people. Like Henry Adams, they cherish the memory of the moment when they left high school with its rigid curriculum and strict discipline to enter their alma mater, there for the first time to enjoy the freedom of youth. Even if they feel like Henry Adams, who wrote in his autobiography that he did not get an education at Harvard, they will think of their student days as something they would not want to have missed. Class and fraternity reunions, alumni meetings, and generous gifts to the alma mater—they all testify to the affection for student days, an affection which in most cases is due to a nostalgic identification of those days with youth.

To students, the University is more than a place for the pursuit of science, a place which keeps itself isolated from communities and presents a cold and impersonal appearance. It is the setting for a student community. There probably is no other institution in which there would be so much of a community among young free people. The students live together in residence halls, fraternity houses, or shared apartments. Even if they live by themselves, they get together with their fellow students in the classroom, during meals, and at a great variety of social events. In a large measure, student life is social life. Friendships made during student days are probably as important as formal instruction. Who could forget a student festivity in the old castle of Heidelberg, or a weekend on Princeton's Prospect Street? Who would not be impressed by the lifelong friendships founded during student days?

The idea that a university is a community of students is as old as the idea of the university itself. The University is not only *universitas scientiarum* but also *universitas scholarium*. As a matter of fact, the latter was the original meaning of the University. *Universitas* means "a whole." When the Pope addressed Christians, he addressed them as *universitas vestra*, "the whole of you." The first use of the term *universitas* in connection with education was *universitas scholarium*, meaning the whole body of students at the medical school of Salerno. Following the practice of merchants travelling together to protect themselves against the hazards of travel and the risks of residence in foreign countries, the students who had come from other cities and countries associated themselves into a *universitas scholarium* in order to better protect themselves against their teachers and landlords, as well as against tradesmen and city authorities. Later on, a similar association was formed by students who had come from Southern Italy, France, and Holland to study law at Bologna. Students at other universities followed suit.

The *universitas scholarium* has existed down to our day. This is quite natural. As was stated earlier, the young feel pretty much lost in the world. They yearn for community. And just as youngsters in general often have associated in youth movements, students have organized within universities. In many respects, the reasons for such organization are similar to those that led to the earliest student associations. Like their predecessors, modern students usually come from outside the town in which they study. There is a good chance that they will be taken advantage of by their landlords, by tradesmen, by those in charge of public utilities such as buses and tramways, that they will be treated arbitrarily by the public authorities. They will organize themselves in order to protect their interests in the local community, be it directly or indirectly through the good offices of the university administration. Of course, students will also organize in order to protect their interests vis-à-vis the university authorities. Interested as they are in instruction, there is reason for them to unite to ensure good instruction. As in the old days, there always exists the possibility that teachers will neglect students or take advantage of them. Furthermore, there are problems with respect to the disciplinary rules of the university, be they concerned with academic or social life, and many others.

As society and universities became more complex, the problems of students increased. This is well reflected in the fact that universities no longer have just academic deans but also deans of students, who are in charge of a great variety of matters. In the University of Chicago, for instance, the Dean of Students "coordinates the University's relations with students, including admissions, recording and reporting, health service, physical education and athletics, the educational and social supervision of residence halls and clubhouses, the direction of social affairs, the control of student organizations and publications, vocational guidance and placement, student aid, the administration of fellowships and scholarships, and of the service function of the Office of Examinations, and of student advisory service in the College, the Divisions, and the Schools." [5] It looks as if the *universitas scholarium,* as a device for the protection of the students, is here to stay.

YOUTH IN THE COMMUNITY OF SCHOLARS

The *universitas scholarium* is not just a community among students but one of students and teachers.

It goes without saying that students organize themselves not primarily for the sake of their protection from townspeople or in order to deal with matters that nowadays generally fall within the jurisdiction of a dean of students. All of these are peripheral to the main concern of the students—learning. Whatever the complaints of students may be, in most cases they are prompted by the desire of creating an atmosphere that is conducive to learning. The facilitation of intellectual pursuits traditionally has been the major rationale for the formation of student communities and for their actions.

Even in the early days of the University, the protection of scholars from landlords, tradesmen, and the public authorities was nothing but a means for a better pursuit of studies. More important was the students' protection from their instructors. This protection did not imply so much physical well-being, which was pretty secure under the laws, but their spiritual welfare and intellectual opportunity. Basically, this meant that there would be no obstruction of learning and no neglect of instruction. The instructor was not to interfere with the scholars' studies and yet was to be available for teaching and consultation. Students requested both the freedom from and the right to be with the teacher. Student protection implied the right to solitude, as well as the right to pursue studies with the teachers, to form with them a community of learning. Were it not for the latter community, the term *universitas studentium* could have been used instead of *universitas scholarium,* implying as it does a greater distance between teachers and students. Eager to learn, but generally not yet learned, a student is less identifiable with a teacher than is the scholar. The community of

[5] Robert M. Strozier, "In Loco Parentis: University Services to Students," in *Issues in University Education,* ed. Charles Frankel (New York, 1959), 124.

scholars and teachers was in a large measure aided by the socratic method which was then prevalent on account of a relatively small number of students.

The development of the community of scholars soon was matched by a similar development among teachers. As a *universitas scholarium* had come into being in Salerno and Bologna, a *universitas magistrorum* was established in Paris. Here teachers organized themselves into a community which guarded its members against the abuses of competitors and saw to it that without proper qualification no scholar could claim the title of master. Other universities followed suit.

Again, the *universitas magistrorum* did not merely imply a community of teachers vis-à-vis the students. It also meant a community of teachers and scholars. Just as scholars felt that for the progress of their education they needed the counsel of their teachers, teachers did not want to be deprived of the stimulation by their students. The latter, sometimes scholars in their own right, would often rise to the rank of master. Thus the student body would continually replenish the faculty, enabled to do so by the latter's efforts.

In the beginning of the University, the relationship between students and teachers was thus a communal, not to say symbiotic, one. Great as the tensions between students and teachers may have been—and often they were substantial indeed—the basic community between students and teachers was never seriously contested.[6] By the fourteenth century, the University was *universitas magistrorum et scholarium,* "the whole of masters and scholars," a name which soon was replaced by the simple term "university."

The community between teachers and students is a natural one. It follows from the nature of teaching and learning and, especially, from the nature of the University as an institution for the advancement of learning and the search for truth.

There exists, of course, a certain community between teachers and students if only because teaching and learning are interdependent, for there can be no teaching without learning and no learning without teaching. Most of us also would agree that the relationship between teacher and student differs from that of a grocer and his customer. While the teacher offers, and the student receives, instruction, as the grocer offers, and the customer receives, merchandise, the former relationship generally is more personal. This by itself, however, does not mean that it also would be more communal. It is conceivable that the better a student and a teacher know each other, the more antagonistic

[6] See Noah Edward Fehl, *The Idea of a University in East and West* (Hong Kong, 1962), chap. 6.

they become. Therefore, there may be less of a community between student and teacher than between customer and grocer. People will argue that this situation exists only in the presence of doctrinaire and intolerant teachers or students, both of which are contradictions in terms. This argument is not without foundation. Still, even in the absence of the antagonism described, teaching and learning alone do not necessarily create a community between teachers and students. Everyone who has been to primary or secondary school, to college, or listened to a lecture, has been aware of it.

The reason for the frequent failure of teachers to establish a community with their students probably is that teaching often is a mere presentation of knowledge. Aside from running the risk of being dull, this kind of presentation unduly confronts the "knowing teacher" with the "ignorant" students. The probability of a community between teacher and students increases when teachers, instead of merely presenting knowledge, strive toward the advancement of knowledge. The teacher no longer appears to possess a monopoly on knowledge, and the student derives encouragement from that fact. Interested in the advancement of learning, students and teachers share doubts about existing knowledge. They form a community in doubt. That community is continually enlivened and consolidated by joint desires and attempts to find the truth. Whereas teaching in the form of a mere presentation of knowledge is prevalent in educational institutions that prepare for the University, teaching and studying in the form of an exploration of the truth and an advancement of learning is characteristic of the University.[7]

Since the collaboration of students and teachers, and its inherent cross-fertilization, will yield scientific results, the *universitas magistrorum et scholarium* is conducive to the *universitas scientiarum*. In turn, since learning is advanced through science, science emerges not only as the youthful means for the exploration of the truth but also as a means for bringing youth into a community with their seniors. The *universitas scientiarum* thus is conducive to the *universitas magistrorum et scholarium*. The concomitance of these two conceptions of the University, their complementary character and interdependence, perhaps account for the fact that imperceptibly the meaning of the University changed from "the whole of masters and scholars" to "the whole of sciences." As the former, the latter also became referred to simply as University.

It is no mere coincidence that modern universities, founded with an

[7] See Lithuanian School Plan, *Gesammelte Schriften,* XIII, 279; Friedrich Schleiermacher, *Gelegentliche Gedanken über Universitäten im deutschen Sinn* (1808), in *Pädagogische Schriften,* ed. Erich Weniger (Düsseldorf, 1957), II, 90ff.

emphasis on a scientific approach, stressed not only research and teaching but also the community of teachers and students. This emphasis was evident in pioneering universities such as Göttingen, Berlin, and Johns Hopkins. Schleiermacher, who, two generations after the founding of the University of Göttingen, was influential in shaping the University of Berlin, felt it was the University's task "to awaken in the noble young men who already possess a certain knowledge, the idea of science . . . in order that they may naturally see everything from the point of view of science . . . and be able to familiarize themselves with every branch of knowledge." Speaking of the "university teacher who is stimulated by living with youths who are full of intellectual curiosity and whom he stimulates in every possible way," Schleiermacher emphasized that "even the most silent and industrious investigator, in his happiest moments, which are those of discovery, . . . must feel like communicating in the most lively and enthusiastic manner and must desire to reveal himself in the spirit of young men. No important university teacher can hold his chair with dignity without having encountered investigations and tasks which demonstrate to him the great value of a community in which everyone is supported by everybody in his scientific pursuits." [8]

In the interview that led to his election as the first president of the Johns Hopkins University, Gilman told the trustees that he would make the university "the means of promoting scholarship of the first order, and this by only offering . . . instruction to advanced students," that he would give professors "only students who were far enough advanced to keep them constantly stimulated." [9] On the twenty-fifth anniversary of the university, Woodrow Wilson, who had received his Ph.D. from Johns Hopkins in 1886, congratulated Gilman for being "the first to create and organize in America a university in which the discovery and dissemination of new truths were conceded to rank superior to mere instruction, and in which the efficiency and value of research as an educational instrument were exemplified in the training of many investigators," and for having "established in America a new and higher university ideal, whose essential feature was . . . the education of trained and vigorous young minds through the search for truth under the guidance and with the co-operation of master investigators—*societas magistrorum et discipulorum.*" [10]

Today, nearly three-quarters of a century later, it is necessary to question whether the community of teachers and students still exists.

[8] *Ibid.,* 95, 99.
[9] *The Nation* (Jan. 28, 1875), XX, 60.
[10] Johns Hopkins University, *Celebration of the Twenty-fifth Anniversary* (Baltimore, 1902), 39f.

The answer, which differs from country to country and from university to university, is on the whole affirmative.

As far as Germany is concerned, the community between teachers and students exists less today than it did prior to World War II. In 1913, Germany had a population of about 67 million and about 79,000 students in 21 universities and 11 institutes of technology. In the beginning of this decade, the Federal Republic of Germany and West Berlin, with a population of about 55 million, had about 200,000 students in only 18 universities and 8 institutes of technology. In 1928, there were 3,050 chairs for about 112,000 students and in 1962, 3,160 chairs for about 200,000 students. The founding of new universities so far has not substantially remedied this situation. It is obvious that the increase of students must depersonalize the relationship between teachers and students and jeopardize the community between them. The community-forming, common search for the truth and advancement of learning in a large measure has been replaced by confrontation between teacher and students. On the other hand, it cannot be denied that there still exists a substantial community formed by the professor and his students. Seminars are still relatively small, and laboratory work is still undertaken by individuals or small groups in close contact with faculty. Most important of all, work on a dissertation still is done in collaboration between the student and his professors, often with just one referee, affectionately called *Doktorvater*.

In the United States, the seminar method, introduced by a few universities toward the end of the last century, has been adopted by most universities. This to a large degree prevented a depersonalization of the relationship between teachers and students. It neutralized the dangers arising from the increase of the student body, noticeable especially since World War II. These dangers were not as great as in Germany to begin with because in the United States the growth of the student body generally was matched by an increase of universities and faculties. The student-faculty ratio is considerably more favorable in the United States than in Germany. Community-feeling also is aided by the fact that in America students are not confronted by a few "chairs." They are not taught only by chair-holding professors, or by full professors, but also by associate and assistant professors. In contrast to the assistants of German professors, assistant professors in American universities hold faculty rank and form a link between students and senior faculty. The community of teachers and students is further aided by the fact that, in contrast to their German colleagues, American professors, even in courses that are not classified as seminars, often use the socratic method instead of lecturing, or a combination of both. Moreover, American professors on the whole are more available to students. Mark Twain's description in *A Tramp Abroad* of the German professor who enters the classroom, talks with prodigious rapidity and energy for an hour, and rushes out of the room and disappears is still fitting today. Aside from some participation in seminars, I talked to a professor only upon graduation from law school when I asked Walter Jellinek whether I could write my dissertation under him. I was quite surprised when in America I saw students after a lecture literally besiege their professors, who gladly conversed with them. American professors often help their students in writing doctoral dissertations to a degree that makes doubtful whether the final product really demonstrates the students' ability to do independent work. There is no doubt that in the United States there exists today what Woodrow Wilson at the beginning of the century called *societas magistrorum et discipulorum*.

YOUTH WITHOUT DEMOCRACY

It is significant that Wilson spoke of the "society of masters and disciples" instead of the traditional "whole of masters and scholars." Perhaps the distinguished student of government and society felt that the traditional term, using *universitas* rather than *societas,* was inadequate and bore within itself the roots of its own destruction. As a matter of fact, the traditional term, while implying community, is silent as to whether and by whom that community is governed. One could answer that "the whole of masters and scholars" is governed by the love and exploration of the truth. Ideal as that answer may sound, it presupposes that men are angels and does not dispel the specter of anarchy among men as they really are. Masters and scholars may have different conceptions of the truth and how to discover it. If each group proceeded on its own, the community of masters and scholars, which is most conducive to science, could fall apart. A genuine community needs a government. It is possible that his realization that the term, *universitas magistrorum et scholarium,* implied no government led Wilson to speak of *societas magistrorum et discipulorum.*[11] For *societas* usually is a specific partnership or association, a legal community with some kind of government, be it only a contract. Even if used more generally, it means an association that is more organized than *univer-*

[11] Cf. Woodrow Wilson, *The State* (Boston, 1889), 17f.

sitas, which can mean the whole of everything irrespective of organization or government.

Ideal as "the whole of masters and scholars" may sound, it was not meant to be a disorganized community from the beginning. Scholars may have been "roving scholars," but the community of scholars as it developed in Salerno and Bologna was tied to a specific institution. From this connection with an institution follows the position of the scholars vis-à-vis the masters. Since the community of scholars preceded that of masters, it could be expected that the combination of both would be called *universitas scholarium et magistrorum.* Instead, it was called *universitas magistrorum et scholarium* and for good reason. Naming the masters first and the scholars second indicates the primacy of the former over the latter and expressed what had been evident already in Salerno and Bologna. No matter how much scholars may have organized themselves into a community, they were not running schools like Salerno and Bologna. On the contrary, they were under the jurisdiction of those schools which were represented to a large degree by the masters. Whatever the rights of the scholars were, they did not entitle them to be enrolled in a specific institution of learning. Such an enrollment was a privilege (*privilegium*) granted by the institution. By enrolling, the scholars entered into a contractual relationship with their school. They voluntarily agreed to subject themselves to the latter's rules and regulations. In doing so, they recognized the authority of the masters over themselves in matters of education. Ideally, the University may have been "the whole of masters and scholars," in the sense of an unorganized, ungoverned community. As realized institutionally, it was the whole of masters and scholars, in which the masters came first. It was *universitas magistrorum et studentium,* or, as Wilson put it, *societas magistrorum et discipulorum.*

The subordination of students to teachers is not surprising. It follows from the very purpose of the community of masters and scholars and from the nature of education. Since the purpose of the academic community is to explore and to discover the truth, that community must be organized in a way that promises the achievement of that aim. From the teleological nature of education follows the superiority of the relatively educated part of the academic community over its relatively uneducated part. The faculty must direct the students. While it is conceivable that students will have insights that are denied to erudite professors, these cases are exceptional. Generally, teachers, being more learned and having greater experience in scientific methods, will know more about, and be more representative of, the truth than students. Letting students guide their teachers would amount to letting those who know less guide those who know more, to elevating ignorance over knowledge. It would contradict the very meaning of guidance. Furthermore, it would mean that those who have not mastered existing truths and hardly are representative of the truth would lead those who have mastered such truths and are more representative of the truth. It would reduce the search for the truth to a paradox.

Faculty authority over students by no means reduces students to servants of the faculty. It merely insures that students will serve the truth as much as professors. Citizenship in the academic community precludes the service by any group or individual to another because academic citizens must serve the truth only. This does not preclude, however, that students would have to respect their teachers. The very fact that students serve the truth must make them eager to learn because service to the truth normally increases with learning. Furthermore, since "student," derived from Latin, means one who is eager to learn, students must respect learning and, consequently, those who are learned. This is the basic law governing the relationship between teacher and student. It is the basis of the academic order. In respecting his teacher, a student does no more than his teacher, who will respect the leading authorities of learning and often proudly consider himself their student.

Respect for the authority of learning and for those who are learned does not imply a loss of individuality. God's will that men shall be free by knowing the truth is not comparable to the will of men as it was advocated by Rousseau, who believed in the dogma that the will of the people is the will of God. Whereas according to Rousseau the individual becomes absorbed by the general will, the academic citizen, while being a member of the academic community, retains his individuality. For in contrast to Rousseau's society, academic society has no general will that could absorb the individual. Wilhelm von Humboldt, who strongly favored a community of teachers and students, could well emphasize in his Lithuanian School Plan that "only in the University can the individual find, by and within himself, the insight into pure science," and that for this individual effort, "freedom is necessary and solitude helpful." Although the society of teachers and students is conducive to the search for truth, it has as its prerequisite the integrity of its citizens' individuality.

Even though the nature of the University as an educational institution required its organization as a society of masters and disciples from the very beginning, the authority of the former over the latter originally was not too conspicuous. Later on, it increased. This was

77

due mainly to the advancement of science and the coming of mass education.

Much as the *universitas magistrorum et scholarium* had become *universitas scientiarum* in the beginning of the modern era, and much as this may have augured the advancement of science, the relationship between students and teachers for some time did not differ much from what it had been in the middle ages. The teacher was a master and respected as such. At the same time, the student, who generally was well prepared when he entered the University, was enough of a scholar to lessen formal distinctions in rank. In practice, the community between master and scholar was quite close. The former seldom had to "discipline" the latter. The body of knowledge was small. It was fixed, concrete, organized. A master generally had "mastered" his field or fields of instruction. He often knew what was going on in other fields and had an idea of the university of sciences. He was able to present students with a body of knowledge that was not too complex. With good reason, the student could hope that one day he would master science. "Science is the organisation of thought," Whitehead said.[12] The relatively clear organization of thought as it existed prior to the stupendous advancement of science in recent generations made the pursuit of science relatively simple. The students were not likely to get confused, and there was little chance that they might lose their bearings. As a result, there was little need for the masters to emphasize their authority.

The expansion of the sciences changed the situation. The proliferation of scientific disciplines resulted in the increased disciplinary functions of teachers. The latter no longer were called masters and for a good reason. They no longer mastered their own discipline, let alone other disciplines and their position in the university of sciences. Professors merely profess to be students of their particular discipline, seldom of more. "It is no accident that an age of science has developed into an age of organisation," we read in Whitehead's essay. Again, it should be added that the many new discoveries that are being made constantly topple existing organizations of thought and necessitate new ones which are only to be toppled again by new discoveries. In earlier times, the scientist was rooted in one organization of thought which occasionally would be amended. The modern scientist is thrown from one scientific organization into another. Before he has comprehended one, he must familiarize himself with a new one. Eager to discover, the scientist has become the pawn of discovery. While all this may be in the interest of science and may speed up the discovery

[12] Whitehead, "The Organisation of Thought," in *Aims of Education,* 154.

78

of the truth, it also confuses—especially those who are beginners, the students. They often feel lost. More than ever before, they need the guidance of their professors. Perhaps this prompts American students to remain at one university, a practice which is becoming more and more common in Europe. The professors must keep the students on the path of science and lead them along that path. For the sake of the advancement of science, professors increasingly must emphasize their authority vis-à-vis their students. As "an age of science has developed into an age of organisation," an age of super-science is bound to develop into an age of super-organization. With the advancement of science, professorial authority is bound to become a super-authority. The scientific imperative requires that the University, after moving from *universitas magistrorum* to *universitas scientiarum* and from a university to a multiversity, be a society in which professors must discipline their disciples more than ever before.

This necessity is intensified by modern trends toward mass education which have opened the gates of universities to men and women for whom they previously were closed. In saying this, I do not have in mind the admission of those who on account of their social background seldom would have studied in earlier times. The pursuit of the truth does not depend upon social status. While education is a privilege, no social privilege ought to frustrate its availability. The chance of becoming a natural aristocrat in the Jeffersonian sense ought not to be hindered by a nostalgia for artificial aristocracy. We have in mind the presence in universities of young men and women whose educational background and intellectual performance in earlier times would not have entitled them to the privilege of higher education. While some of them work hard, many are pseudo-students who are anything but eager to learn. Now there always have existed people of that type in universities. The "eternal student" who goes on and on "studying" without ever taking an examination has long been a standing joke at European universities where a liberal interpretation of academic freedom includes the student's right not to study. These students used to be the exception. Since they had to pay their fees and living expenses, the invisible hand of which Adam Smith spoke took care that there were not too many of them. Today, the situation is quite different. Generous government subsidies make it possible for many unworthy students to crowd universities. Unfortunately, university officials all too often abet this regrettable situation. Only a little over a decade ago, financial aid was given to outstanding students only. Only they would be honored as scholars and fellows, titles that suggest a deep commitment to learning and an intellectual proximity to the faculty.

Today mediocre students not only receive scholarships which enable them to retard research and the education of good students; they often get as much aid as do the good students, depriving scholarships and fellowships of their meaning as a reward for excellence. The feeling that they are entitled to aid regardless of their performance leads them to lessen their efforts, to drag on and on, and to delay their examinations.

In this situation teachers must attain and exert more authority vis-à-vis students than in the old days. To students who enter universities less prepared than their predecessors, professors must appear as greater authorities than previously. Toward them, as well as toward the lazy students, teachers must use their authority by urging them on in the pursuit of learning. But the exercise of their authority cannot stop here. It must also be used to eliminate unworthy students from the academic community. In doing this, teachers not only fulfill their obligations toward the society which guarantees their academic freedom and often supports them materially; they also serve the end of that freedom and support, namely, the advancement of science and the pursuit of the truth. In preventing an overcrowding of universities with unworthy students, they will refine the community of teachers and students and enable them to more easily see the light of the truth in clarity.

From the above it follows that the academic community cannot be democratic. If the purpose of that community is to discover the truth and to attain clarity, there can be no room in it for anything that could frustrate that purpose. Much as a democratic society can be conducive to academic aims, democracy within the University is sufficiently served by the collegiate system that prevails among the faculty.[13] And useful as student participation in the exploration of the truth can be, student participation in the formulation of academic policy generally must be detrimental to the aims of the University. Even in the absence of the principle, "one man, one vote"—which on account of democratic thrust is likely to become accepted, once first steps toward democratizing the University are taken, and would enable students to outvote the other members of the academic community and bring about an academic paradox—student participation is fraught with danger.

Denying students the kind of participation in the governmental process that is enjoyed by ordinary citizens is necessitated by basic differences between academic and political communities. Citizens of

[13] Schleiermacher, *Gelegentliche Gedanken über Universitäten,* 123f.

80

the latter, irrespective of their education, can participate in the political process because that process is to yield nothing but a consensus on how they want to live. They are free to make their decision. In a way, they are free to create their own truth. Determined subjectively, that truth is something occasional, something relative that can change from nation to nation. On the other hand, academic citizens are interested in the truth that is the same everywhere. It is not created by them. Nor is it something relative that they can determine according to their subjective tastes. It is something absolute, something objective, that is revealed on account of their determination to find it. It derives not from a yearning for convenience but from the often inconvenient labor of constant inquiry. For the discovery of the truth, education is quite relevant. While there are exceptions, that discovery generally will be reserved to what Max Weber would have called the aristocracy of scientists.

Although the University as a haven of science should not be controlled by aristocrats of birth, it must be run by an aristocracy of scientists in order to give birth to an aristocracy of the mind. It would be a paradox if the aristocrats-to-be, the students, could run the aristocrats who are, the teachers—if those who have not yet arrived could order those who have arrived. It would defeat the mission of the University if students were permitted an influence which could be detrimental to the discovery of the truth and to scientific progress. Although there is no harm in some of the synergetic devices that exist on campuses—such as student representation for certain purposes, the elective system, course-rating booklets, student newspapers, and peaceful demonstrations that do not interfere with learning—students as a matter of principle ought not to determine the formulation of academic policy, matters such as the curriculum, the handling of courses, and the hiring of faculty, lest they contradict the rationale for their being in the University.

The University shares with youth a desire to find identity through truth. Yet, as a symbol of clarity, the University is the antipode of youth, which is a symbol of confusion. Youth is in the University to progress from confusion to clarity. Permitting students undue influence in running the University must confuse the University. It must deprive youth of an institution that is ideally suited to the alleviation of their problems.

4

YOUTH AGAINST UNIVERSITY
From Clarity to Confusion

YOUTH IN DEMOCRACY

To modern students, their exclusion from the government of universities must appear strange indeed. Most of them have been used to sharing in policy-making throughout their lives. To them, democracy is no longer merely a form of government in which they are entitled to participate when they come of age. It is a way of life they have experienced since childhood. Democratic activity no longer means something legal, implying political privilege. It means something natural to all men. The young no longer grow toward democracy. Democracy has grown toward them.

In the not too distant past, growing up meant shutting up. In their homes, children were told what to do and were expected to obey. If they were nasty, they were put in their place. Children generally had no voice in the formulation of parental policy. The story has been told of a Roman emperor who admitted that his son was the most powerful man in Rome because his wife did whatever the son wanted and he, the emperor, fulfilled all her wishes. Even if this anecdote were true, it would describe an exception to the rule. Up to our time, children and youths generally recognized the authority of their parents and knew they had no right to participate in family government.

The situation was similar in educational institutions. Until recently, students in elementary and secondary schools considered themselves under a disciplinary order controlled by school administrators and teachers, in spite of the pedagogical changes since Locke and Rousseau. Even "progressive education" generally was still balanced by the upbringing students had received at home. Although students would occasionally squabble with school officials, they usually did not think of running things. Recognizing and accepting the educational nature of schools, they seldom demanded participation in school government. Entering universities, they generally considered the latter educational institutions on a higher level and did not expect to share in their government. Furthermore, students enjoyed more freedom in universities than in preparatory schools. Free to select their field of study and to indicate their preferences within the university marketplace, they did not clamor for a voice in running universities.

The recognition of universities as educational institutions, implying the students' acquiescence to their exclusion from the government of these institutions, was bound to change once earlier stages of education promoted the participation of children and youngsters in policymaking. This situation came about when "the century of the child" was initiated. An important event in this development was the publication in 1945 of Dr. Benjamin Spock's *The Common Sense Book of Baby and Child Care.* The best-selling work of its kind, it has had a great impact. By advocating that children be given a stronger voice, it has substantially contributed to the democratization of the family. Published when the United States was becoming the undisputed leading power in the world, its ideas spread not only through the United States but also to many other nations. Child rearing in large measure became "Americanized," constituting an American challenge which in the long run probably is of greater consequence than the one about which Jean-Jacques Servan-Schreiber wrote.[1] A visitor to the United States in the late forties could not help being struck by the strong position of children. What was the exception in Europe appeared the rule in America: children could defy their parents and generally get away with it and have their way. Family life revolved around children. Loving care emerged as a veritable cult of the child whose wishes would influence, and often determine, parental decisions. One had to wonder whether those who then were babies and children later on might become not only a new generation but a new kind of generation. Given the Americanization of other nations, might not large parts of the globe one day be faced with that kind of generation?

The new orientation in child care at home had its impact upon schools. It came to complement the new pedagogy known as progressive education, which originated in the United States as an appendage of the "progressive movement." Just as the progressive movement wanted to expand democracy beyond existing constitutional restraints, progressive education tended to extend democracy to the classroom by loosening existing methods of discipline and by granting students a greater influence in school affairs. John Dewey, the main proponent of progressive education, stated before the end of the last century that "all education proceeds by the participation of the indi-

[1] Jean-Jacques Servan-Schreiber, *Le défi américain* (Paris, 1967).

vidual in the social consciousness of the race. This process begins
unconsciously almost at birth. . . ." [2] His early book, published in
1900, significantly has the title, *The School and Society,* and begins
with a chapter on "The School and Social Progress." To progressive
educators, that social progress was the progress of democracy from
limited to unlimited democracy and its adaptation to the classroom.
This is evident in Dewey's *Democracy and Education,* published at the
time Woodrow Wilson thought of making the world safe for
democracy. Its pages "embody an endeavor to detect and state the
ideas implied in a democratic society and to apply these ideas to the
problems of the enterprise of education." They provide for "a critical
estimate of the theories of knowing and moral development which
were formulated in earlier social conditions, but which still operate, in
societies nominally democratic, to hamper the adequate realization of
the democratic ideal." [3]

After the democratization of the classroom had progressed and
Dewey himself in the early thirties had bewailed "educational
confusion," educators began to wonder whether the realization of the
democratic ideal in the classroom might not hamper the realization of
the educational ideal. At about the time they seriously considered
moving away from progressive education in schools, however, parents
began to accept Dr. Spock's methods of child rearing. These methods
deprived those who opposed democracy in the classroom of
something that had counteracted the democratization of
schools—namely, the inclination of children to obey their teachers, an
inclination due to their having been brought up in the "old-fashioned
way." Dr. Spock's common sense baby and child care, arguing for a
community among children and parents and participation of the
former in the government of the family, pulled the rug from under the
feet of common sense educators. Although that rug had become
shabby from the passing feet of progressive educators, pulling it away
increased student power further.

Democratic trends in home and school were nursed by democratic
trends in society, trends which also favored the young. While children
and teenagers today generally have no right to vote, the young have
good reason to believe that they will soon be enfranchised. The
history of the suffrage is a history of extending the suffrage. Just as the
suffrage was extended from property owners to nonproperty owners
and from men to women, it has been extended to the young. For
instance, in France after some experiments in the decade following

[2] John Dewey, "My Pedagogic Creed" (1897), *Education Today* (New York, 1940), 3.
[3] John Dewey, *Democracy and Education* (New York, 1916), v.

the revolution, the Constitutional Charter of 1814 provided for a minimum voting age of 30. The constitution of 1830 and the electoral law of the following year lowered that age to 25, and in 1848, it was reduced to 21. A law proposed for Germany in 1849 put the voting age at 25, and that age prevailed under the Second Empire. For the elections to the National Assembly of Weimar, those over 20 could vote, and this remained in effect under the Weimar constitution. Whereas the Bonn Basic Law raised the voting age to 21, there is a movement under way in West Germany to lower that age to 18, which has been successful on state and federal levels. In the United States, the voting age generally is 21. In newly admitted states such as Alaska and Hawaii, however, it is 19 and 20, respectively. In 1944, Georgia reduced it to 18. Kentucky followed suit in 1956. The movement toward lowering the voting age in other states and in the District of Columbia continues.

From a democratic point of view, the lowering of the voting age is as natural as the abolition of property and sex qualifications. Meaning government by the people, democracy in the last analysis means government by as many people as possible, by all the citizens of a community. In an absolute sense, democracy implies the participation of youths and children in the governmental process. Any legislation providing for a certain minimum age for voting must appear as arbitrary as legislation providing for a certain minimum of ownership, taxes, or for a certain sex or race. In another generation, people will probably deny that our time was democratic because teenagers were not permitted to vote, just as people today say that the nineteenth century was not democratic on account of property qualifications. Still later, people may well assert that a time in which children could not vote was not really democratic. The "century of the child" thus is a natural phrase for a century that has been characterized by a democratic thrust which, after the elimination of property, race, and sex qualifications, has become directed against age qualifications and is likely to abolish those.

Parents giving children permission to influence their decisions, teachers letting students participate in running schools, and legislators granting permission to youths to vote—they all have extended democracy to the young and thus in a way have raised the young to the status of adults. It is not surprising that the young, having received quasi-legal and legal backing in their quest for self-government, have become self-conscious, and that youth no longer is an ordinary new generation but a new kind of generation which differs from previous generations in cohesion, numbers, and outlook.

Prior to World War I, Mendousse could still complain that adolescents were considered "big *children* or young *men,*" not youths.[4] At that time, there were "young people" rather than "youth." While here and there they would organize themselves into youth movements, these movements constituted but a small part of the total of young men and women. By contrast, modern youth has become an independent social group, enough of a specific category to be declared in 1967 by *Time* magazine the "Man of the Year." That "Man" is about to become a superman.

Youth has considerably expanded within society. Biological acceleration and the prolongation of education have numerically increased youth. About half a century ago, youth was understood to comprise those aged 15 to 20. Today it comprises those from about 13 to 25. This means that the fraction of youth within the entire population has more than doubled.[5] Furthermore, the population explosion in large parts of the world has enlarged the youth population. In Canada and the United States, those under 25 already constitute one-half of the population. It is expected that by 1980 every second inhabitant of the earth will be under 22.

The increase in numbers and cohesion, implying an increase in power, has influenced the outlook of youth. The attitude of youth used to be primarily one of questioning, not of action. Today questioning generally results in action and often violent action. Formerly, although the turmoil and uncertainty inside individuals occasionally became evident in loud and boisterous behavior, it generally would not seriously attack or challenge the existing order. Such attacks and challenges may have been contemplated by youth movements; however, since these movements constituted only a small fraction of the total youth population, were diversified in their aims, and often neutralized one another, they did not pose a serious threat to the existing order. Today the situation is different. While insecurity and the search for identity still plague individual youths, they are now comforted by a feeling of being part of a powerful new kind of generation, a fairly cohesive group which they can hold on to, which can represent them and promote their aims in the outside world. Having become a pressure group similar to adult pressure groups, youth seem intent on using their power. Because of their new strength, their former compensatory attitude which had manifested itself in occasional individual displays of disruptive behavior has become an overly compensatory attitude, manifesting itself in individual or group actions which are often characterized by violence.

This new attitude, in a large measure the result of the permissive-

[4] Mendousse, *L'âme de l'adolescent,* i.

[5] See Pierre Bertaux, *La mutation humaine* (Paris, 1964).

ness of parents, teachers, and legislators, is aided by the overly youth-oriented attitude of adults, an attitude that perhaps is motivated by a desire to assuage the bad conscience that derives from a realization that their permissiveness toward the young was a mistake. Adult orientation toward youth is an outstanding feature of modern Western society. It often amounts to a youth cult which has all the marks of a fetish. Whereas prior to World War I, youth generally looked up to their elders as examples to be imitated, now it is often the other way around. Formerly, adults naturally longed for the days of their youth and yet knew how to grow old gracefully. Today they consider growing old something to be ashamed of and neurotically crave to stay young, going out of their way to give themselves youthful appearances. Whereas formerly youths aped adults, adults now ape youths. Although the former behavior is not too serious because youth grow up, the latter behavior can be disastrous because adults have no natural escape from their condition. As puerilism is a psychiatric symptom for the mental disorder of an individual, the present widespread youth cult could well indicate a mental disorder of society. At any rate, that cult makes adults the laughing stock of those who are naturally and sanely puerile. It must reduce whatever respect the young still hold for their elders. Thus youth are powerful not only because adults have increasingly lifted them up to their own level but also because adults have increasingly descended to the level of youth.

Democracy embraced the young in the home, in schools, and in public life to a degree that justifies the statement that youth have been used to a democratic way of life from childhood on. Rousseau's ideas are close to being realized. The author of *Émile*, favoring the emancipation of children and youths from adults, also was the author of the *Contrat Social*, which favored absolute democracy. He was quite consistent. Democracy being basically insatiable, the march of democracy cannot stop until everybody can participate in government. It had to emancipate the young for the democratic process.

YOUTH RIOTS

This, then, is today's university student: he is a youth who has been used to having a voice, and often his way, in his home and school. He has received, or is about to receive, the right to vote. He is surrounded by a youth cult. He sees "those over 30," who try to imitate him, who in his eyes appear to be degenerate, getting physically weak and about to capitulate to him. Like youths of earlier generations, he may still feel lonely; however, he no longer is alone the way they were. He is aware that he belongs to a powerful, new kind of generation, and he derives assurance and comfort from this fact. Whatever his background, color, and orientation, whatever the degree of his desire for change, and his support from university personnel, the modern student senses power. Yet, in universities, he is denied power. Used to participating in decision-making from childhood, he must think that he is being used—and abused. Universities must appear to him as institutions in which all power is concentrated in the hands of those who run them. Perhaps knowing John Adams's statement that "power is always abused when unlimited and unbalanced," that "absolute power intoxicates alike despots, monarchs, aristocrats, and democrats, and jacobins, and *sans culottes*," [6] he would be wary that power has intoxicated those who govern universities, that it is abused by them. Will he counter by using and perhaps abusing his power against universities?

While I disagree with Burckhardt's statement that "power is of its nature evil"—it all depends upon who exercises it—and feel that Plato's philosopher-king might be a good form of government, there is also truth in James Madison's observation that "power in human hands is liable to be abused" and in Lord Acton's words that "power tends to corrupt and absolute power corrupts absolutely." [7] Has power corrupted modern students?

The answer depends on a variety of factors. First of all, I shall assume that corruption through power implies an abuse of power with ill consequences. Of course, this need not be so. A do-gooder can indulge in exercising power and still be a blessing to mankind. Corruption by power can manifest itself in illegal exercises of power and can, given the fact that law is only a moral minimum, maximize that minimum. Acting *ultra vires* of the law thus can well be in accordance with higher justice and morals, although it is likely to jeopardize legal security. However, the concern here is not with corruptions that bring about something good but with abuses that harm education. Such abuses can be classified into those which are characterized either by student passivity or activity.

Students could abuse their power by simply being lazy. This is nothing new and many people feel it ought not to be taken too seri-

[6] John Adams, *Defence of the Constitutions of Government of the United States of America* (1778), in *The Works of John Adams,* ed. Charles Francis Adams (Boston, 1850–56), VI, 73, 477.

[7] Burckhardt, *Reflections on History,* 86; James Madison to Thomas Ritchie on Dec. 18, 1825, *The Writings of James Madison,* ed. Gaillard Hunt (New York, 1900–10), IX, 232; Acton to Bishop Creighton, April 5, 1887, in *Historical Essays and Studies,* ed. Figgis and Lawrence (London, 1907), 504.

ously. As a matter of fact, the German concept of academic freedom, *Lehr- und Lernfreiheit,* implies that the registered student has the right not to study. This concept, which outraged Fichte,[8] partly originated when universities clamored for students who paid their own way and contributed to the revenue of universities and university towns. Since the number of students then was small and since the lazy students seldom deprived others of the opportunity to study, *Lernfreiheit* was perhaps justified. Furthermore, it gave students who had to work their way through the university a chance to take a job during class hours and study at night. Aside from the last consideration, the situation is different today when universities often cannot accommodate all those who want to study and when many students receive financial aid from private and public funds. Moreover, the public may be hurt insofar as laziness may spread and lower academic standards. This is a problem in Western universities today which is especially serious in view of the persistent raising of standards in Communist countries. It could result in the free world's being "outbrained" by the authoritarians, in jeopardizing not only Western security but also the free search for the truth. Nevertheless, indefensible as student laziness is and incompatible as it is with the concept of academic freedom that implies the moral duty to study, I shall not further elaborate on it here. The lazy will take care of themselves as much as the diligent. Although the probability that the lazy will be weeded out is no longer as great as it used to be even under the relatively strict American system, student passivity for the time being does not seem to constitute as imminent a danger to the University as do certain activities.

I am concerned here with activities that interfere with learning. Student pranks do not fall within this category. Caution, of course, must prevail toward them and a strict line should be drawn between genuine pranks and behavior that can jeopardize learning. Moreover, we must guard against activities that parade as pranks and actually are motivated by sinister designs and violate criminal law. Still, we must be careful not to attribute those designs to everything students do and always keep in mind that students, after all, are youth. The pranks described in the famous student jails at Heidelberg must have been plain fun, and the world would be poorer without them. Often justly denounced for going too far, pranks can be useful outlets for youthful exuberance. As a natural relaxation, they can be conducive rather than detrimental to learning.

It is also doubtful whether student power is abused if it is employed to improve existing conditions. While the end does not justify the

[8] Fichte, *Ueber die einzig mögliche Störung der akademischen Freiheit* (1812), *Sämmtliche Werke,* VI, 449.

means, the means appears to be more justifiable if the end is good. Student actions against universities thus could be defended if universities stand in need of reform. In that case, the employment of dubious means might be more warranted than most people believe. To determine whether students abuse their power it is necessary, therefore, first to examine whether universities have swerved from their ideal.

In many respects, universities must be a great disappointment to students. This disappointment is likely to be not just another disenchantment in a chain of letdowns the individual has probably experienced ever since entering the critical age of youth. It could well be the major disappointment of his life because of the great hopes one puts in universities. During the first hard years of youth, when he was looking for his identity and became increasingly confused instead, universities must have appeared to him as veritable incarnations of freedom and wisdom, institutions that would stabilize him and give him peace of mind. He knew that once he entered a university he would be free from the strict curriculum of the preparatory school. He sensed that not only would he be freer but also wiser. No longer would he just accumulate a certain amount of knowledge; he would participate in the exploration of the truth and in the expansion of knowledge. The often narrow approach of the preparatory school teacher would be replaced by the open approach of the university professor. He felt sure that in the university he would find—at long last—his identity and his bearings.

Having matriculated, he knows he will study a special field to prepare himself for a specific profession. "Still, the university with its aura of tradition represents to him the unity of all branches of learning. He respects this unity and expects to experience it, and through it to arrive at a well-founded *Weltanschauung*. He wants to arrive at truth, wants to gain a clear view of the world and of people." [9] The university he enters appears to him as a haven of clarity, the realization of the ideal. He feels that it can be the greatest thing on earth.

Unfortunately, he soon finds out that it is not, that it is a quite earthly institution with many shortcomings. Instead of a noble and ennobling humanity, he finds ordinary and often vulgar humans. Instead of the search for the truth, he finds a great deal of fraud. Instead of liberty, he finds restrictions and intolerance. Instead of universality, he finds narrow specialization. The divine idea of the clear and scientific quaternion, *universitas, libertas, veritas, humanitas,* is confined to confused and evasive human quarters. Academic life turns out to be not a glorious but a vicious circle. In universities, the humane impera-

[9] Jaspers, *Idea of the University*, 39.

tive of ennobling humanity through hard work, humility, and sacrifices, often is frustrated by degrading human foibles such as laziness, vanity, arrogance, and the conveniences that go with them. The latter show that there are many men in academic life who do not belong there.

The academic career often does not attract the best people. Many of them are not as intelligent and as diligent as those who want to become doctors, lawyers, and businessmen. They are lured by vacations rather than by obligations. After they have mastered the chores of their dissertation, they are unable or unwilling to produce a piece of scholarship again. They concentrate on teaching, which requires putting in about half of the time other professions require and offers generous vacations on top of it. There is a sad truth in one of George Bernard Shaw's *Maxims for Revolutionists*: "He who can, does. He who cannot, teaches." Although it probably would go too far to say that professors concentrating on teaching degrade their Ph.D. to a ph.d., they often are petty, pedestrian men who derive a sense of their own importance from facing those "who do not know"—their students.

Aside from laziness, vanity often prompts people to enter an academic career. This motive is especially strong in Germany where the university professor has enjoyed high prestige and where something like an academic aristocracy has developed. While the social position of the American professor still cannot be compared to that of his German counterpart, there have been trends toward raising his prestige, especially since Professor Woodrow Wilson became President of the United States and Franklin Roosevelt formed his Brain Trust. American academic achievements justify these trends. Although it is easier to become a professor in the United States than in Germany because of the considerably greater number of universities, many a German *Ordinarius* has been a *Durchschnittsprofessor* whose scientific achievements would not have qualified him for a full professorship in leading American universities. The glamour-seeker basically is out of place in a university whose paramount task is truth-seeking, since the desire for glamour in the eyes of the public is likely to hinder efforts to search for the truth. Scientific effort usually is an unglamorous, lonely ordeal which perhaps will be rewarded by having come close to the divine, an *Erlebnis* which more than compensates the scholar for the glamour that goes with public approval.[10] Unwilling to make intellectual sacrifices, the scientist must sacrifice many of the so-called pleasant things of life.

If the scholar is productive, his work often will be characterized by timidity. This, again, has its source in human factors as well as in the

---

[10] Weber, *Wissenschaft als Beruf,* 573.

circumstances of his formative years. The American graduate student who plans to enter an academic career often is more timid than the undergraduate. Many undergraduates impress by their aggressiveness and enthusiasm. Graduate students seldom do. They consider themselves more dependent on their teachers, whom they feel in a large measure determine their careers. The situation is similar to that of German candidates for academic life. Many a *Privatdozent* has received his *venia legendi* by being on good terms with his professor rather than through scientific achievement. Often, he has merely shown greater perseverance than his colleagues to whom a *Habilitation* was refused by doing academic coolie work such as digging out data for the professor's research, helping the professor teach and grade papers, and by doing all sorts of personal chores for him, including grocery shopping for the professor's wife. Under these conditions, many subservient men will become professors from whom daring and challenging contributions to learning cannot very well be expected. They form the academic middle class which often seems to be the backbone of universities.

If those who fail to contribute to the advancement of learning through research would simply reconcile themselves to their failure and concentrate on teaching, the situation would still be bearable. They usually are not that modest. For the sake of their own prestige they usually oppose hiring men who are much worse than they. On the other hand, they keep out anyone who is, or could be, a little better and more productive. "The excellent are instinctively excluded from fear of competition, just as the inferior are rejected out of concern for the prestige and influence of the university. The 'competent,' the second-rate, are selected, people who are on the same intellectual level as oneself." [11] What is worse, incumbent second-raters not only keep away outstanding people but also try to drive or "ease" out colleagues who have pushed ahead of them.

All too often they succeed in doing so through a behavior that is unbecoming among colleagues or by virtue of their administrative power. For, regrettable as it is, administrative power in universities often is in the hands of those who failed or were about to fail as scholars. Unable to receive recognition in their profession, they crave being a big fish in the small pond of their university. Goethe commented on the sickness of universities as compared with independent research: "Here as everywhere learning advances quietly or dramatically, while those professionally concerned with it are not really interested in it at all but are merely interested in money and power." [12] Perhaps that is a generalization. Still, it applies to quite a few members of the academic profession. Shaw's statement could well be expanded: "If you can't

[11] Jaspers, *Idea of the University*, 71.
[12] Quoted in *ibid.*, 73.

teach, become a dean, and if you can't dean, become a president." Just as in public life where failures often turn to politics, academic failures often turn to politicking within the university and to seeking administrative posts. But whereas politicians are controlled by an electorate which can prevent a catastrophy by recalling, or not re-electing them, a university may be saddled with administrative officers until they have ruined it. This danger exists especially in the United States where administrators generally are not elected periodically and hold office during a considerably longer period than their European counterparts. In universities, the ideal of finding the truth is thus matched, and perhaps overmatched, by the practice of exercising po-litical power. The power of knowledge often is challenged and de-graded by the power that results from the failure to push the frontiers of knowledge. The contempt and arbitrariness of many administrators toward scholars is too well known to need further elaboration. Max Weber's warning to those who contemplate an academic career is as valid today as it was fifty years ago: "Do you think you can stand it without becoming embittered or being destroyed, that year after year mediocrity after mediocrity moves ahead of you?" [13]

The vicious circle continues. The ideal of seeking the truth is not only paralleled by the practice of seeking power but is also mocked by malpractices of seeking money. Having failed in honest research efforts, many professors are quite successful in their devious search for money. This is evident, for example, in applications for research grants, applications which often are devised not with a view toward doing the investigations proposed but with a view toward improving the probability of receiving a grant. Applications are often geared to what one thinks foundation and government officials are interested in rather than to what one wants to do, if anything. If the money comes through, a lot of it is likely to be wasted and the end result will be meager, if there are any results at all. In the latter case, professors often will have the nerve to tell those who made the grant that while much progress has been made on the proposed project it has turned out to be more complicated than was originally anticipated. They will ask for a renewal of the grant and will likely get it. Administration officials often support these operations through negligence, conniv-ance, or outright complicity. As a matter of fact, fund-raising by ad-ministrators often demonstrates the behavior of professors on a larger scale. Another dubious procedure is that of inducing offers from other institutions. The professor who does not excel in scholarly productiv-

[13] Weber, *Wissenschaft als Beruf,* 572.

ity often indulges in handshaking with astounding results. He will receive offers through the good graces of his friends, often second-raters who will favor adding another one to their company. Having received the offer, he will run to his dean and ask him to match it. Even if the offer is from a noncompetitive institution, the dean often will make concessions, partly because his friend is a "nice and competent man to have around," and partly because keeping him is more convenient than hiring someone else. This encouragement generally will induce the professor to continue to be unproductive as a scholar and to concentrate on the money game instead.

The liberality toward that game often is not matched by a liberality toward academic freedom. As was shown above, in Western democracies that freedom has been so generally recognized that it seems to be part and parcel of university life. In practice, however, the situation is often quite different. Although professors, administrators, and trustees will pay ample lip service to the idea of academic freedom, under the surface there is a great deal of unofficial intolerance. Professors are frequently expected to conform to a certain set of beliefs. Austrian universities have been known as strongholds of Catholicism; their Swiss counterparts, as places where one had better belong to the Reformed Church. In spite of the ideas behind the founding of the universities of Göttingen and Berlin, a certain conservatism for some time was characteristic of German universities. This has been changing. Still, conforming to the prevalent climate always has brought advantages. The same is true of American universities, where the climate is one of "progressive" liberalism. The situation bewailed in the early William Buckley's *God and Man at Yale* still prevails. Ever since "liberals" wrested academic freedom from those governing universities, it has become risky for the individual not to agree with their kind of liberalism.[14] More and more, that type of liberalism seems to have become accepted throughout the Western world, an aspect perhaps of the Americanization of universities Weber envisaged.[15]

Laziness, vanity, and arrogance, the seeking of and corruption through power, the elimination of excellence, the negation of the search for the truth, devious pursuits of material things, intellectual sacrifices, and the absence of freedom—all can be found in modern universities. To these must be added a high degree of compartmentalization and specialization. Whereas the latter are not necessarily as detrimental to the exploration of the truth as is often believed and may serve the aim of the University, the student is unlikely to see it

[14] See Russell Kirk, *Academic Freedom* (Chicago, 1955).
[15] Weber, *Wissenschaft als Beruf,* 568.

this way. Young and inexperienced, he will feel lost in a labyrinth of cold and impersonal classifications and disciplines. Unable to fit himself into any classification, he will often lose his self-discipline. He will find it hard to adjust to an environment where everyone seems to forget that a multiversity is just a means for the achievement of the University and not an end in itself. Having come to the university to find his identity, he will fear that the multiversity depersonalizes him and reduces him to a little wheel in a big apparatus.

In short, his familiarization with university life may well come to the student as a great shock since university practice may appear to be the negation of the ideal University. His belief in that ideal, his youthful idealism and urge to improve the world, may become channeled into condemnation of university practices and a zest for university reform. Sensing their power, youth may want to use it, for the sake of the University against those who run universities. Given the abuses of university personnel, the use of student power, as long as it is directed to remedy these abuses, can hardly be an abuse of power. Employed the right way, it cannot be immoral or illegitimate. It may not even be illegal.

If one examines recent student riots, one finds that they have rarely been directed against the kind of university abuses described. While there have been complaints about depersonalization and dehumanization, in general these riots have tended to further the abuses I have denounced and to favor things that are detrimental to the idea of the university.

First of all depersonalization is not as bad as it has been depicted. Aside from the fact that professors generally are more available to students than has been conceded, a certain distance between those who teach and those who learn follows from the nature of education. The university professor is not a spoonfeeder and the university student should consider it beneath his dignity to be spoonfed. Lower forms of education are more or less exclusively concerned with teaching and provide for frequent personal contacts between teachers and students. Universities are supposed to advance, not merely present, knowledge. The university professor must devote a large portion of his time to research. Although his research efforts often will be made in community with students, he is necessarily unavailable to the large mass of those whom he meets in the classroom only. Student insistence that relationships with professors be more personal and that teaching take preference over research inevitably reduces universities from institutions of higher, to those of lower, education.

96

Dehumanization presupposes an incompatibility with the idea of the university, an idea which implies *humanitas*. Even admitting that university practices exist which are incompatible with that idea, many of the programs of today's student rioters are also incompatible with *humanitas*. These programs may be human; however, I cannot discover much that is humane in the free speech movement of Berkeley, a movement which propagated the use of four-letter words, in the "horror commune" at the Free University of Berlin which propagates free love and dwells on long-winded and boring discussions of orgasm, and in "love-ins" and other forms of sex craziness and vulgarity that have come to light in student behavior. When Joan Baez indicated that there is not much *humanitas* in breaking into a university president's office and smoking his cigars, she was right.

Other programs are equally dubious. Increasing requests to lower standards of admission and of examinations, generally motivated by the desire to avoid hard work, need no comment. Suggestions for new courses and programs of study on the face of it often seem to be justified. Although they are likely to expand the multiversity at the expense of the University, they may well advance learning. Furthermore, they are in tune with the development of university curricula which have expanded throughout history. The introduction of new programs, however, is risky if these courses cannot be effectively taught, either because of a lack of qualified teachers or adequate literature. University instruction presupposes certain standards. In the absence of such standards, the students are unlikely to get much out of new courses, no matter how much they may have wanted them. Equally dubious are demands to "commit" universities. For the reasons stated above, committing a university to "social functions" and to "community work" usually runs counter to the University's proper aim of exploring the truth irrespective of the pressures of the environment. Similarly, demands for a political commitment of a university are incompatible with the idea of the university. Universities may be the homes of "schools of thought" that criticize and compete with one another, but they cannot be committed to one particular ideology, popular as that ideology may be. An ideological university is a contradiction in terms. One of the most vocal of today's demands is student power. While that power may be useful in fighting malpractices, it ought not hurt the realization of the ideal University, something I am afraid it has been doing. Because of the nature of education as a process which implies the subordination of students to teachers, student power for the sake of student power must be more dubious than the principle *l'art pour l'art*.

The platforms of today's rioting students suggest that their advocates are not the best of students. Good students would rebel against the practices I have denounced. Rioting students hardly mention them. This is not surprising since, in many respects, rioting students can be considered malpracticing counterparts of malpracticing professors and university officials. Just as professors shrink from the tribulations of research, student rioters often shrink from their obligations to study. As unsuccessful professors become operators with administrative ambitions, unsuccessful students turn to operating student demonstrations. The professor's vanity is flattered when he becomes an administrator, and the egos of radical student leaders, who often are not popular in the student community, are flattered when they become big activists in small groups of rioting students. As professors favor second-raters, rioting students favor egalitarianism. As administrators demonstrate arrogance toward faculty, student activists show arrogance toward faculty and administrators. As professors and administrators play the money game, rebelling students complain that financial aid is insufficient, that all too few fellowships include generous travel allowances and other indications of affluency, that all too little money is spent on student amusement. Just as professors no longer are interested in the expansion of knowledge but present the knowledge available to them, student radicals offer their own, ready-made truths to fellow students and university personnel. Professors often look askance at a colleague who does not share their kind of liberalism; students act as if they have a monopoly on liberalism. In many respects, modern student rebels mirror what is bad in university establishments. Although they speak of improvement, they are likely to make things worse.

Although rioting students reflect many of the attitudes of university administrators and professors, they differ from them in some of their means. Their actions constitute a higher dimension of the behavior of university officials. Administrators and professors—who, like students, do not behave uniformly and fall into categories such as regents, trustees, administrators, senior and junior faculty—block the advancement of learning by refraining from research, by hiring and promoting second-raters, etc. Still, while the rewards they earn for their dubious behavior may well discourage and seduce those who fulfill their duties toward the University, they do not actively prevent their more honest and more diligent colleagues from promoting the advancement of learning. Furthermore, they do not interfere with instruction. Since one hopes that every faculty member, be he excellent or second-rate, will know more about his subject matter than his students, his students generally will be able to get all the information they want and are able to consume.

The situation is different in the case of student rioters. They do not merely frustrate the advancement of learning by avoiding research and instruction, by persuading or inducing others to be lazy or to go on strike, etc. They actively prevent research and instruction by exercising pressure upon students, faculty, and administrators. They physically obstruct the ordinary process of learning through such devices as sit-ins, the occupation of offices, classrooms, laboratories and libraries, and the outright destruction of educational facilities. Their activities are often more straightforward than the devious behavior of administrators and professors and appear to be defensible in institutions that are supposed to promote the truth and presumably must appreciate honesty. Actually, they do greater harm to the pursuit of the truth than does the more passive behavior of administrators and professors. They prevent the process of learning, whereas the latter generally only delay that process. The behavior of administrators and faculty is not generally incompatible with academic freedom to the point of jeopardizing that freedom. Student riots, characterized by pressure and violence, are incompatible with academic freedom. Furthermore, the behavior of university personnel has not generally endangered the university order, which is a prerequisite for free learning. Student riots have endangered that order.

While student complaints about academic malpractices can help to make and keep universities havens for clarity in which students can escape the trials of youth and mature to master the tasks of adult life, student riots as we have experienced them are likely to accomplish exactly the opposite. They will make universities veritable cauldrons in which students will become increasingly confused. Out to destroy universities, they could wreck the cream of youth. In a word, by turning against universities, youth turn against themselves.

UNIVERSITY ORDER

At a time of student unrest it is vital for universities to rebuke radical attacks. The effort is worthwhile. Whatever the malpractices in today's universities may be, universities in general still come close to realizing the ideal University. At least, they have an enormous potential to do so. They are worth preserving.

For their preservation, universities must maintain order. In doing so, they enter another phase of their past which has been characterized by a défense of their integrity against popes and kings, as well as against bourgeois and proletarian powers. A defense of university order is clearly a legitimate task. The substance of that order is a highly moral one, whether one considers the ends of universities or the means to achieve these ends. The exploration of the truth is truly humane, as is the freedom to explore. As the exploration of the truth is an absolute and perhaps unattainable goal of universities, freedom is a comprehensive means. Freedom implies not only the right to seek the truth on the basis of rational evidence but also through speculation, irrational as it may appear. In a famous dispute at the height of the Darwinian controversy, the pathologist Virchow pleaded that unproved hypotheses should not be taught as true, that professors should stay within their fields of competence and never express possibly dangerous beliefs without taking into consideration the consensus of their peers. The biologist Haeckel replied that no line could or should be drawn between objective and subjective knowledge and that science would best advance through the clash of correct and incorrect opinions. The latter attitude came to prevail even before Virchow, who had ridiculed the suggestion that tuberculosis was caused by living organisms, was proved wrong by the discoveries of Robert Koch. Universities have been shelters of a comprehensive academic freedom.

Liberal as universities may have been, their attitude might not have amounted to much in the absence of effective protection of academic freedom within them. Such protection traditionally has been ensured by university order. Universities are not loose *ad hoc* organizations whose moral pursuits give them an aura of legitimacy. They are concrete legal orders. This means, first, that they enjoy a certain degree of independence from the public power; second, that within the limits of their jurisdiction, they ensure order. Just as the individual's academic freedom from outside powers must be complemented by an internal academic freedom which implies discipline for the sake of production, the independence of universities from the government implies an obligation to order their internal affairs in a way that guarantees a maximum advancement of learning in freedom. This is the *jus strictum* of the university order.

Wherever there is strict law, there is the possibility that it will be too strict. Legal orders have often come under attack for being too restrictive. The history of the law is a history of "the eternal recurrence of natural law," [16] which questions whether existing law is compatible with higher or "juster" law. Basically, men's recourse to natural law has been a good thing. As Faust says in his study, laws "like an eter-

[16] Heinrich Rommen, *Die ewige Wiederkehr des Naturrechts* (2d ed; München, 1947).

100

nal disease, linger on from generation to generation." Jefferson, the great American advocate of education, put it this way: "I am certainly not an advocate for frequent and untried changes in laws and constitutions. . . . But I know also, that laws and institutions must go hand in hand with the progress of the human mind. As that becomes more developed, more enlightened, as new discoveries are made, new truths disclosed, and manners and opinions change with the change of circumstances, institutions must advance also, and keep pace with the times. We might as well require a man to wear still the coat which fitted him when a boy, as civilized society to remain ever under the regimen of their barbarous ancestors." [17] Have university orders become so antiquated as to be oppressive and justify student rebellion?

There are indications that they have become antiquated. The cap and gown, worn in the middle ages, to some students symbolize this fact. *Unter den Talaren, Muff von tausend Jahren* ("Under the academic folds, a thousand years of mold") read a sign carried by protesting German students in front of an academic procession. Especially in Europe, many aspects of university life seem to be out of date. We need think only of the sacrosanctity of traditional faculties and the reluctance to create new ones; of the skepticism toward new approaches and new disciplines; of the entrenchment of institutes and the autocratic methods of running them; of the hardships of the "apprenticeship" of assistants, etc. Although the situation is better in the United States, American universities are still not free from archaic features.

However, it is debatable whether these features are as harmful as they are often depicted. There is value in respecting the old, especially in the present time, which seems to favor change for the sake of change. Even Jefferson would probably have opposed the modern urge to change laws. It must never be forgotten that while he knew that "laws and institutions must go hand in hand with the progress of the human mind," he also left no doubt that he was "certainly not an advocate for frequent and untried changes." Changes in university institutions probably are less justified than changes of the laws and constitutions in general. Even though it is useful to remind people of the eternity of law and justice, as is done by judges wearing cap and gown and wigs, the adjustment of laws and constitutions to current needs hardly can be avoided. Since it is generally believed that the aim of laws and constitutions in a large measure is social engineering, they are bound to change, especially in our democratic age of legislation.

[17] To Samuel Kercheval on July 12, 1816. *The Writings of Thomas Jefferson* (Mem. ed; New York, 1903–4), XV, 40f.

On the other hand, the aim of universities is the unhindered search for the truth, a constant goal that ought not to be influenced by new conditions. Whereas judges today must obey the legal imperative defined by the democratic ruler irrespective of their desire to cling to higher concepts of justice, professors should consider themselves only under the academic imperative of searching for the truth and usually do not desire anything else. Their search could well be more successful in university orders that have proved their value for some time than in atmospheres of innovation, especially if these orders are tolerant of, and even further, experimentation.

Even if one agrees that many university features are antiquated and ought to be eliminated, rebellion against the university order would not be warranted unless these features turn out to be oppressive. It should first be said that oppression by universities can only mean the oppression of those who are already in universities. Admission policies, for example, cannot be oppressive because university jurisdiction does not apply to those who are not yet registered. Furthermore, "oppression" should be understood in the classic sense—namely, infringements upon existing rights of the individual. The refusal to give students additional rights after they have enrolled or to extend certain favors and conveniences to them—such as admission of coeds and friends, adopting a new calendar or new study program, building a student union, establishing laboratories or computer centers or athletic programs—are not oppressive acts. Defined in ordinary terms, oppression means arbitrary and unlawful deprivation of life, liberty, and property. By that definition, the university order is clearly not oppressive. It would not even occur to most students that universities deprive them of life, liberty, and property. I do not want to apply ordinary standards in the case of universities, however, although an application of higher standards does not justify the use of the term "oppression." In contrast to political societies, universities are liberal by definition. Their liberal image causes entering students to expect a greater degree of freedom from universities than from other institutions. Even if one applies high standards, however, it cannot be said that universities are oppressive. To the contrary, students in many respects are freer than people outside the universities. They are deferred from military service. They can demonstrate peacefully without having the permission of the police. In many instances they will be able to damage or destroy university property without being asked to pay for damages or without being criminally prosecuted. What is more, they enjoy these privileges because they are registered as students, irrespective of whether they actually study or not. Today's students are, as far as their freedom is concerned, a *jeunesse dorée*.

Even if students did not enjoy the liberties just mentioned, and even if universities did deprive them of their rights, universities still could not be considered oppressive because of the principle, *volenti non fit injuria.* The relationship between student and university is a voluntary one from which no injury can result to the student since he need not enter and is at any time free to leave the university. A university does not try to conceal anything from prospective students. It has a certain reputation. It informs the public about itself through regularly published and distributed catalogues which provide data on calendar, curriculum, facilities, fees, extracurricular activities, etc. It gives additional information to inquiring students in writing or orally. Thus, before a student applies for admission, he has had ample opportunity to inform himself about the university, its rules and regulations. If he has not done so, it is his own fault. When he applies, he knows that the university will turn down many applicants, hopes to be admitted, and considers admission a privilege. If he is admitted, he is still free to collect further information on the university and to compare its offerings with those of other universities that have admitted him. He can reject or accept his admission.

By accepting, the student admits his preference for a particular university. He voluntarily enters a contractual relationship with that university. In entering that relationship, he recognizes the university order, its rules and regulations. Whatever these rules and regulations may be in detail, the university order by definition turns around what can be considered the hard core of the educational contract—learning. This contract implies that the student will refrain from anything that in any way interferes with the regular process of learning as it is conducted by the university, or with academic freedom as guaranteed by the university order. While that order often will permit him to stay away from classes, and even to induce others to stay away voluntarily, he is not permitted to prevent others from learning through an obstruction of teaching, research, studying, or administration. Student pressures of any kind, polite or rude, have no place in institutions which can fulfill their task only in an atmosphere of freedom. *A fortiori,* student violence, often in conflict with criminal law, cannot be condoned. Universities may extend privileges to the *jeunesse dorée*. They are not sanctuaries for a criminal youth.

The *jus strictum universitatis* applies to both state and private institutions. While the former often differ from the latter in their admission policies, the legal relationship between students and universities is similar. Their strict law does not make universities oppressive. Aside from the fact that the principle *volenti non fit injuria* precludes oppression even if university demands were exacting, the educational contract is usually not demanding at all as far as the basic freedom of the student is concerned. Although universities generally would profit from the student's commitment for a number of years, they do not require such a commitment. The student can leave not only after an academic year, but from semester to semester. Often he will even be permitted to leave in the middle of a semester without material disadvantages. In contrast to most contractors, universities often will not insist on a strict observance of the principle *pacta sunt servanda* and not require the student to show *rebus sic stantibus*.

No particular university order is thus imposed upon a student. He can quit and change to a university that is more to his liking. The latter opportunity is especially great in the United States where there are not only an enormous number of universities but also great variety among universities. There are private and public, denominational and nondenominational, men's, women's, and co-ed schools with substantial differences in academic standards, approaches, and other aspects of orientation. Even in nations where universities are state-controlled and are rather similar, such as in Germany, the possibility of choice still exists. Since the conditions of the educational contract are rather generous for the student, their strict observance must be expected as long as he is in a university. *Noblesse oblige*—both ways.

The requirement that students strictly observe the university order does not preclude student protest. Universities are places of protest by definition. Aiming at the discovery of the truth and the advancement of learning, universities are outposts of protest against existing achievements. Student participation in that protest, much as it may be directed against their professors and administrators, is a prerequisite for a true university. The right of student protest goes even further. Students can protest if they feel the university does not fulfill its contractual obligations. While this generally will be difficult for the students to prove because university catalogues often reserve the right to change, there still may be legal cause for protest. The right of students goes still further. They may also protest against the fulfillment of contractual obligations. It is quite conceivable that once the educational contract has been entered, students might want to change it, and the university might want to go along. In this case, however, the university must examine whether the change is desired by all the students or just by a fraction. If a majority of students protest for change, the university must not go along unless the change is agreeable also to the minority of students. Otherwise, the university would not fulfill its contractual obligations toward the minority. *A fortiori,* a protest by a student minority should only be followed if the majority approve. Whether they constitute a minority or a majority of the student body, protesters have no right to impose their will upon their nonprotesting fellow students by unilaterally bringing about a change of the educational contract. Whatever student protests there are and for whatever reason they are undertaken, they must not interfere with learning.

Protests are only justified if they are provoked by the university. To protest against a university because of someone else's error or because of some general dissatisfaction is like S hitting innocent U because he was hit by A or is unhappy about B. For example, the failure of President Johnson to fulfill some of his campaign promises, much as it may have justified protests against his administration, in no way justified riots in universities. No matter how much universities may be involved in war research—something academic freedom entitles them to do—they cannot be blamed for the policy of the President of the United States, nor can the students whom riots deprive of the opportunity to study, for which they have paid tuition. The failure of the two major parties to nominate presidential candidates that are to the liking of the New Left, much as it may justify protests against these parties, does not justify university strikes which deprive students of the instruction they are entitled to. Failures of the German federal government, much as they may cause protests against that government, do not justify riots in universities which are not under federal, but under state, control. The independence of German universities being what it is, such failures would probably not justify action against universities even if they were controlled by the federal government.

If one now turns to ways and means to defend the university order against student riots, it will not be necessary to dwell long on preventive measures. Causes for legitimate complaints, like the ones described above, incompatible as they are with university morality, must be abolished. Other preventive measures follow from the nature of universities as legal orders. First, a university order must be complied with by university officials themselves by their setting an example for the students. Rules, regulations, and requirements must possess a certain stability because frequent changes are likely to result in legal insecurity and pave the way for anarchy. If university officials indulge in overthrowing rules, regulations, and requirements by constantly changing them, or if they disregard existing rules and regulations, students cannot be expected to have a high regard for the university order. That order must be strictly enforced and arbitrariness must be avoided. Universities can demand much from students. As soon as they treat students arbitrarily by extending little and big favors here and there, students will wonder about the ethics of university personnel who are supposed to serve the truth.

If strict enforcement of the university order is the guiding principle for the prevention of student unrest, it must also be imperative for the quelling of riots. Since Western society is threatened with a breakdown of law and order, universities must prove their élitist character by giving examples of how to preserve law and order. This is not an easy task in view of the fact that universities today are little islands surrounded by the waves of modern democracy and by pseudo-liberals who tend to denounce everything favoring law and order as "illiberal." It must not be forgotten, however, that the defense of the university order is the defense of a genuinely liberal order which by definition is more liberal than most other orders, including the political order. Therefore, the existential rule of liberalism must apply: the more liberal an order, the more determined must be its defense through a strict enforcement of the laws.

Since the university order is a legal order, the proper means for its defense are legal means. Universities must formulate detailed emergency plans to prevent their actions being improvised or arbitrary. Such plans must provide for the procedures of university action and for sanctions against students. Uncompromising in their policy to maintain law and order, these plans still can, depending upon the degree to which rioters violate criminal law, build erring students a bridge enabling them to return to the academic fold. Taking the case of an occupation of a building, the emergency plan must provide for the following steps. First, ask students to leave the building within a period which can reasonably be expected to permit a short discussion of the university's request. Second, if the students refuse to comply with the request, serve them with a court injunction which will bring the support of the law-abiding public behind university authorities. Third, if the injunction is not complied with, force compliance by calling in police. Fourth, discipline, expel, and bring criminal charges against the guilty. Of course, the obligation of students increases with special trusts the university may have put in them. For example, if a student has teaching obligations, then already his refusal to teach because he wants to participate in a strike called by student leaders may justify the university's cancelling his teaching contract.

The successful handling of an emergency can be a university's finest hour. Faced with the moment of truth, a university can demonstrate that there is no "moment" of truth for an institution that serves the truth because truth and the search for it are eternal. In a riot, a university can confirm what universities have proved throughout history—namely, that it is an able defender of academic freedom not only from forces without but also from forces within. In a riot, a university can rise above formidable obstacles for the realization of the humanistic ideal through a maintenance of the university order.

The main burden of this task will fall upon the chief executive of the university. Experience so far has shown that many presidents and rectors have failed, often so pitifully that one wonders how they could have become chief executives to begin with. It has proved my thesis of the often low caliber of administrators. If someone cannot master the hardships of scholarship, there is reason to doubt whether he can master the hardships of student riots, for both require toughness and the willingness to make sacrifices. If someone is insufficiently committed to the exploration of the truth, he is unlikely to be sufficiently committed to the protection of the free exploration of the truth by others. Student riots, then, having demonstrated many an administrator's inability, offer an administrator a golden opportunity to show his ability. In a riot, he can show that he is more than just an egotistic superior of underlings. He can demonstrate that he is a *defensor pacis universitatis*. He can show that he is sovereign, for to be sovereign is to be sovereign in a state of emergency.[18]

Exercising sovereignty, a university executive can be firm with a good conscience. He need not fear being called illiberal, for firmness in the preservation of the university order cannot make him an oppressor. Since a university order is an order within, and subject to, the political order, it is devoid of means of oppression. In the last analysis, the power of a university administrator is smaller than that of a judge and that is small enough. He needs a judge for an injunction and depends upon the police for its enforcement. As a matter of fact, an administrator's firmness is conducive to freedom because the preservation of the university order is the preservation of a liberal order. The liberalism of a university order is evident not only in its ends and means but also in its constitution. All of its constituents, students as well as members of the university establishment, are in it of their free will. The university order is one of the few actual examples of a social covenant. Its preservation means the fulfillment of a freely concluded educational contract. It is as legitimate a task as any because it honors

[18] Cf. Carl Schmitt, *Der Hüter der Verfassung* (Tübingen, 1931).

the dogma *pacta sunt servanda,* a principle which has so generally been
considered the supreme principle of the law that Anzilotti even felt it
was also the first imperative of international law.[19]

ORDER, RIOTS, AND DEMOCRACY

As clear and simple as the preservation of the university order is
from a legal point of view, in practice it is an arduous task. It is doubtful whether insistence upon the principle "contracts must be fulfilled"
can be effective at a time which is characterized by a general erosion
of that principle. As democracy has moved toward an extension of the
suffrage through increasing abolition of property qualifications, governments have become indifferent, if not hostile, to property rights. As
liberal democracy has been replaced by social democracy, emphasis
upon the obligation of contracts has been replaced by trends toward
easing that obligation, be it through inflationary methods or more direct measures in favor of debtors.

Since Western governments, complying with the will of the majority, have increasingly permitted exceptions to the principle that contracts are binding, people cannot be expected to have much respect
for the obligation of contracts. Furthermore, this progressive destruction of the sense of obligation was to bring about a conviction that society has ever-increasing obligations toward people. Since legislation
has freed more and more debtors from more and more debts and enlarged the number of "vital" commodities which cannot be distrained,
more and more debtors could reasonably expect to be freed from
more and more obligations and to be guaranteed an increasing number of vital commodities. In the end, they could claim to be taken care
of by the government or society and to be provided with an ever-increasing standard of living. Nondebtors have followed suit with such
demands. As a result, Western societies have been moving toward
welfare states where people think society owes them a living irrespective of their efforts. If they do not get what they expect, they become
discontented and move toward breaking the law and challenging the
established order. The present breakdown of law and order, usually
reflected in crimes against property rights, is in a large measure the
natural consequence of so-called social legislation. Individual citizens
cannot be expected to respect property rights if the government has

[19] Dionisio Anzilotti, *Corso di diritto internazionale* (4th ed.; Padova, 1955), I, 43, 53ff.,
66ff., 84, 154.

108

consistently disregarded these rights and destroyed public trust and all sense of obligation.[20]

Today's students have grown up in this atmosphere. Rioters are the children the welfare state has released. It must not be overlooked that student riots in Western democracies started in places that were especially generous—Berkeley and Berlin. Berkeley had the best university in an educational system which is probably more generous to students than any other system in the United States. Similarly, the city of Berlin has done more for students than any other German city. Furthermore, students in Berlin enjoy the unique privilege of being exempted from military service—a fact which seems to belie the idea that campus unrest is due to the draft. Aside from the peculiar tie-up of welfare-statism with riots in Berkeley and Berlin, that tie-up also seems to exist more generally. Riots in Germany and the United States—the nations where campus unrest appears to be the most serious—began only after the respective federal governments had started generous programs of aid to education, making student life more comfortable than ever before. These programs also seem to have whetted the appetite for more financial aid, for demonstrations of discontent, for violence—all of which seem to be matched mainly by a slackening of academic efforts.

That acts providing for federal aid to education, such as the *Honnefer Modell* and the United States National Defense Education Act, seem to have achieved exactly the opposite of what they were supposed to raises questions not only of the propriety of taking taxpayers' money for what in the last analysis amounts to a weakening of national security but also of whether universities should handle student unrest by themselves. While I have consistently favored free government and feel that universities should be independent from governments, I also believe that the independence they enjoy through the government's protection obliges them to aid, and not to endanger, the survival of a free society. Universities must not permit themselves, and must not be permitted, to become risks to national security.

Student riots should not be discussed without weighing the possibility of their being desired and promoted by foreign nations interested in sapping the strength of the West. In social democracies it is often considered poor taste to point to the dangers of communism. Especially in academic circles one all too often becomes aware of the truth of Raymond Aron's statement that communism is the opium of the intellectuals. The mere mention of the possibility of Communist threats usually provokes angry reactions by those whom Wilhelm

[20] See the author's *In Defense of Property,* chaps. 4 to 5.

Röpke called anti-anti-Communists.[21] Often anti-Communists are accused of being Fascists in spite of the statement by the martyred Kurt Schumacher that Communists are red-lacquered nazis. Still, I do not want to commit another *trahison des clercs*[22] but abide by the academic imperative and express my opinion irrespective of popularity. The dangers posed by today's student riots are so serious that all possible causes must be examined, including that of a Communist conspiracy. It must always be kept in mind that while suspicions do not prove guilt, they also do not prove innocence. However, I do not want to accuse but merely raise a few questions.

It is, of course, beyond question that riots disturb law and order and work into the hands of those who want to undermine and destroy our way of life. Since this has been the confessed aim of Communist nations, student riots without any doubt aid Communist designs. I also do not question that many students are unaware that their rioting helps communism and that they do not suspect the organizers and leaders of riots to be agents of foreign powers.

There is, however, the question whether such agents are operating. It will be answered that a man like Rudi Dutschke could not possibly be a Red agent because he fled the Ulbricht regime and has continually denounced that regime and its Russian counterpart. All that may be true. On the other hand, since someone denouncing the West German establishment will not get anywhere with West German students unless he also denounces the establishments in East Germany and the Soviet Union, and since it is in the interest of Ulbricht and Moscow that an instigator succeeds in turning West German students against their government, the question arises whether Dutschke was actually asked by Ulbricht to pose as a refugee in order to be more effective in his activities. This could be a tactical retreat for furthering strategic ends, as was suggested by Lenin. Dutschke's denunciations of Communist establishments have not hurt those establishments. On the other hand, his fight against the Free University, West German universities, and the Bonn regime has been quite effective.

Had Cohn-Bendit restricted himself to fighting de Gaulle and praising the Soviet regime while haranguing his fellow-students amidst red flags, he probably would not have got far. As it was, he also denounced the Soviet establishment and thus broadened his appeal with French students. It must be asked whether the condemnation of his activities by the French Communist party and by Communist-con-

---

[21] Wilhelm Röpke, "Umgang mit dem Bolschewismus" (1959), *Wort und Wirkung* (Ludwigsburg, 1964), 91.

[22] Cf. Julien Benda, *La trahison des clercs* (Paris, 1927).

trolled labor unions was not prompted by the desire to increase his general appeal, in order that the existing regime might be undermined more effectively. Again, Cohn-Bendit's attacks against the Soviet Union were futile. His actions against de Gaulle nearly brought down the Fifth Republic. If they did not bring down France, they certainly brought down the franc. Another tactical retreat for strategic gains?

In contrast to Dutschke and Cohn-Bendit, whose zest for demonstrations does not seem to be matched by a desire to conclude their studies and who seem to strive toward the Marxist ideal of the professional revolutionary rather than Humboldt's ideal of the educated man, Herbert Marcuse is a scholar. He wrote major works long before student riots started. He does not seem to be too happy about the publicity he has received as the philosopher of the New Left and appears to be proud of being denounced by the Communists as well as by conservatives. Yet, while I would not think of denying him the free expression of his opinion, one might ask whether his denunciations by Communists might not be prompted by the Communist desire to make him acceptable to larger segments of the public and thus to increase his influence in furthering destructive activities.

The questions raised about Dutschke, Cohn-Bendit, and Marcuse must be asked about many students and professors who denounce the establishment that brought them forth as children of social democracy turned into its Frankenstein's monsters. At the same time, there are many old-time promoters of the welfare state who meant well but now have come to realize the truth of John Adams's statement which this author has emphasized ever since the beginning of the New Frontier: "Property is surely a right of mankind as really as liberty. . . . The moment the idea is admitted into society that property is not as sacred as the laws of God, and that there is not a force of law and public justice to protect it, anarchy and tyranny commence." [23] Like Sidney Hook, they now try to unhook themselves from responsibility for student riots.[24] Those whom they have often treated high-handedly and ridiculed for opposing the march from limited to unlimited democracy must now not retaliate in kind and cynically remark, "I told you so." Faced with a clear and present danger to law and order and survival, conservatives and classic liberals must join those who have favored modern variations of liberalism in order to quell a radicalism which can only make things worse, even though some people might compare this to joining Russia against China. In doing so, however, they must never forget that the alliance for overcoming the radical fringe of the

---

[23] John Adams, *Works*, VI, 8f.
[24] See Sidney Hook, "The Barbarism of Virtue," *PMLA* (1969), LXXXIV, 465.

"liberal" establishment can be an *ad hoc* alliance only. That alliance must not let them accept the dubious sides of the establishment. Otherwise radicals, irrespective of what they may achieve through violence, will at least succeed in attaining one of their aims: the elimination of conservative attacks upon establishments, establishments which make radicalism possible and which without substantial revisions are likely to do so in the future.

While an *ad hoc* alliance between classic and modern liberals can succeed in temporarily halting student riots, it probably cannot, by concentrating its efforts on situations in universities, prevent riots more permanently. Student riots are not merely a university matter but manifestations of a more general social malaise. They cannot be eliminated unless one goes to the root of the evil and heals the malaise itself. An essential aspect of that malady is the degeneration of limited into unlimited democracy, of liberalism into the pseudo-liberalism of socialism and the welfare state, characterized by disrespect for contracts and property. This development, like that of political romanticism, began during the French Revolution, which initiated increasing challenges to law and order by never-ending replacements of customary law through legislation. While a legislative order can be as much of an order as a customary one, legislation by virtue of its innovating character is bound to introduce instability, make law and order something relative, and bring about disrespect for law and order, even if it mainly transmutes traditional law into written norms. Once traditional law is legislated away, this disrespect will snowball and make radicalism inevitable.

An important prerequisite for an enduring peace in universities is, then, the restoration of law and order in Western societies. It must start with a re-affirmation of the bases of the law, such as the protection of contracts and property. This means that social democracy must move toward a genuinely liberal democracy. In view of the fact that the trend has been exactly the other way around, this will appear to many as turning the clock back. Actually, it is setting the clock right because the deterioration of a democratic order into the anarchy which we have experienced has been moving us toward the backwardness of barbarism. Once a democratic order is restored in which freedom is again safe under law, academic freedom will again blossom in universities. In lieu of riots leading youth into confusion, universities will again fulfill their timeless mission and lead youth into clarity. *Veritas et lux.*

DEMOCRACY, UNIVERSITY, AND YOUTH
Conclusion

Democracy today, in view of its advance and general acceptance in Western nations, constitutes a serious threat to the idea of the university. Universities must do all they can to secure the survival of that idea from democratic inundation. By virtue of their character and tradition, they seem to be well suited to this difficult task.

Throughout history universities, pursuing the humanistic aim of freely serving the truth, have been striving toward the realization of the quaternion, *universitas, libertas, veritas, humanitas.* There probably are no other institutions which would have combined freedom and order as naturally and demonstrated so clearly that, just as humanistic aims can be achieved only in freedom, freedom presupposes order.

In a way, universities are microcosms of constitutional governments which protect the freedom of the individual to pursue humane ends. It is probably no mere coincidence that the history of constitutionalism begins at about the time the first universities were founded, that the growth of constitutionalism runs more or less parallel to the growth of universities, and that universities generally have promoted constitutionalism by educating their students in the spirit of freedom and by defending freedom from popes, kings, popular demagogues, and majorities.

The threats to universities in modern democracies are often overlooked. Most democracies profess to be constitutional democracies. They appear as macrocosms of universities, as political orders which are so similar to university orders that, it is believed by many, they cannot well be at odds with them. This kind of reasoning is deceptive, however. Since the fight for constitutional government in a large measure was a fight for an expansion of democracy, it is frequently

113

overlooked that democracy, much as it can be conducive to constitutionalism, can also be detrimental to it. While men perhaps can be better protected in democracies than under other forms of government because self-government is unlikely to be oppressive, freedom seems to be more vulnerable in democracies because it is open to attacks from more sides. In monarchies, freedom is threatened only by the monarch. The monarchical order usually is such that no threat through anarchy need be feared. Much as it may be increased unduly at the expense of freedom, the monarchical order is so strong as to prevent a breakdown of law and order. On the other hand, in democracies freedom can be threatened not only by the ruling majority or a democratic leader but also by the licentiousness of individuals. There can exist a degree of permissiveness which destroys the order necessary for freedom. The one does not preclude the other. In many nations, the march of democracy has produced a degeneration of constitutional democracy into an absolute majority rule which is characterized by a permissiveness detrimental to law and order. In modern democracies, universities must be alert not only to restrictions by the government but also to destruction by those who have no respect for law and order. They must wage, and actually have been waging, a war on two fronts. Their situation seems to be more precarious today than it was when they just had to defend themselves against government interference.

When Max Weber, a strong believer in democracy, pleaded 50 years ago to keep democracy out of the universities, he may well have foreseen the democratic threats I just described, threats which became evident a little over a decade later. The year *Science as a Profession* was published, the Weimar Republic was founded under the first democratic constitution Germany had had. It was too democratic for its own good. Introducing social rights next to classic liberal rights, it soon demonstrated the vulnerability of democracy. After the Depression, constitutional democracy was threatened by executive dictatorship and anarchy. Political factions fought it out in the Reichstag, in the streets, and in universities, which increasingly had become places for political debate and controversy. In the end, Hitler arose and through *Gleichschaltung* streamlined the universities into his system.

Haunted by the spector of National Socialism, the men who drafted the Bonn Basic Law amended many shortcomings of the Weimar constitution under which Hitler had come to power. Yet it remains to be seen whether democracy in Germany is safe. Whereas a decade ago there was good reason to believe that "Bonn is not Weimar," in recent years the question has been asked whether the *soziale Rechtsstaat* of the Federal Republic might not suffer the fate of its democratic prede-cessor after all. The internal development in Germany has been char-acterized by an increasing permissiveness and a drift toward a break-down of law and order, evident especially in student riots. Politics again has entered the universities. Led by the Sozialistischer Deutscher Studentenbund, student rioters have succeeded in paralyz-ing universities.

In contrast to Germany, the United States can look back on a long tradition of free government. Yet she has not been free from the pit-falls of democracy. While the development from limited to unlimited democracy has stretched over many generations,[1] the results of that development have become quite evident in recent years. The drift toward absolute democracy under the New Deal, the New Frontier, and the Great Society, characterized by an increasing erosion of the protection of contracts and property, brought about an increasing permissiveness and a decline of law and order. That decline has been frequently demonstrated by student riots which, generally led by the Students for a Democratic Society, have mutilated several universities. While these riots reflect the general breakdown of law and order that accompanied the march of democracy, they are in a large measure due to the increasing democratization of universities, a process which began at about the time progressive education challenged the classic educational ideal of *paideia.*

When Weber pleaded to keep democracy out of universities, he was thinking of the integrity of science. It may be added that the inde-pendence of universities is not only a blessing to science but also to constitutional democracy itself. Whereas democracy is probably the form of government that can best secure a far-reaching protection of the individual, it can also be the most oppressive form of government. Unlike despotic monarchs or aristocrats who are confronted by the majority of the people and know that at least they are outnumbered numerically, a despotic majority need not entertain such fears. Often narrow-minded in its views, it can afford to oppress minorities and in-dividuals without much fear. Independent universities, geared to uni-versality and liberty, can always mitigate the narrow-mindedness of democratic governments and keep the flame of liberty alive. Further-more, while democracy can be rational, human nature being what it is, democracy can also lapse into an irrational, emotional form of gov-ernment. It can become a government of the big lie. Universities inde-pendent of democracy, devoted as they are to the rational exploration

[1] See the author's *America's Political Dilemma: From Limited to Unlimited Democracy* (Baltimore, 1968).

115

of the truth, can counteract these tendencies. I said that universities can be considered microcosms of constitutional governments. It could be added that universities are of great value in aiding the transformation of the human shortcomings of democracy into truly humane assets. They can be the very institutions that keep constitutional democracy on an even keel and save it from degenerating into extremist perversions. Rather than being interested in democratizing universities, democrats cherishing freedom should, like Weber, shelter universities from democracy.

From all of this it follows that Weber's insistence that the scientist only serve science[2] is not as value-free as some have asserted. The reproach that Weber put a value-free science above humanism is not as justified as many people tend to believe. Weber strongly believed in values, whether he wanted them discussed in the classroom or not. The scientific pursuit itself is a value. There is no discrepancy between *veritas* and *humanitas*. The exploration of the truth, ruthless though it may be and unpleasant though its results may be, is perhaps the most humane task humans can undertake. When Nietzsche feared the advancement of learning at the expense of man, he had in mind an all too technical, specialized advancement that was unlikely to measure up to *veritas* and *humanitas*, not the kind of learning that supposedly is done in the University. Perhaps it has been the universities' misfortune that *Science as a Profession*, published at the height of positivism and considered by some the climax of that school of thought, did not seem to object to such an advancement and no longer emphasized humanistic doubts about learning. Its value-free approach may thus have contributed to the degeneration of science into mere scientism, into a formalistic attitude which has risked dehumanizing science, just as legal positivism has jeopardized justice.

Have universities indeed become dehumanized? Did university teachers, whom Fichte called "priests of the truth" and who Nietzsche hoped would take the place of the priests who had betrayed Christianity and killed God, fail to keep universities humane? If they did, it would not be surprising. Ortega's complaint about the dehumanization of art[3] applies quite generally to twentieth-century life. The barbarian whirlpool may well pull everything under, including the universities. Still, universities have pretty well escaped dehumanization. Insofar as they have not escaped, it is probably for the most part due to the improper introduction of politics into classrooms and to teachers becoming preachers.[4]

[2] Weber, *Wissenschaft als Beruf*, 575ff.
[3] José Ortega y Gasset, *La deshumanización del arte* (Madrid, 1925).
[4] Cf. Daniel Coit Gilman's address, Johns Hopkins University, *Celebration of the Twenty-fifth Anniversary*, 23.

Our restless, occasionalist world, characterized by political opportunism, is interested in having politics on the campus. It is against this trend that Weber voiced special concern when he emphasized that "politics does not belong in the auditorium. It must not be introduced there by students . . . but also not by the teacher." [5] Without doubt, this "disenchanted" many of those who longed for empathy; however, these students would have done better had they studied under professors the way Weber advised them to and not emphatically demanded a *Führer*. A little over a decade later, they had the *Erlebnis* of the *Führer's* Third Reich and experienced the *Entzauberung* of the century.

Their suffering ought to be a warning to today's students. Again, some of our young people complain about the depersonalization and dehumanization of universities. Again, students want to introduce politics into the classroom and are enchanted by the dreamworld of political utopias. Used to affluence, their programs are less moderate than those of their predecessors 50 years ago. It is to be hoped that their greater hopes will not result in greater disenchantments. For disenchantments greater than those provided by Hitler could well mean the end of civilization.

Today's running after "kicks and trips" derives from the cause Weber mentioned when he stated that modern man, and especially youth, find it difficult to fulfill the requirements of daily life, that the running after the *Erlebnis* results from the weakness of being unable to face harsh realities.[6] In this sad situation, one hopes that a searching, confused youth, living in insecure and confusing democracies, will recognize again the clear and clarifying reality of the University and be enabled to face reality. Serving the truth may well give clarity and happiness to youth.

[5] Weber, *Wissenschaft als Beruf,* 584f.
[6] *Ibid.,* 589.